Kuan Yin Buddhism:
The Kuan Yin Parables, Visitations and Teachings

Kuan Yin Buddhism

This book is dedicated to my extraordinary family, who every step of the way, encouraged its completion.

KUAN YIN BUDDHISM:
The KUAN YIN PARABLES,
VISITATIONS AND Teachings

2019

Kuan Yin Buddhism

Cover Art:
https://commons.wikimedia.org/wiki/File:Kuan_Yin_(192598053).jpeg

Kuan Yin Buddhism: The Kuan Yin Parables, Visitations and Teachings
©2019 Hope Bradford
ISBN: 9781695491304
Imprint: Independently published

All rights reserved. No part of this book may be used or reproduced in any manner whatsoever without prior written permission from the publisher, except where permitted by law.

Disclaimer: The content of this book is intended to be general only and not as any form of advice, diagnosis or therapy and is not intended to replace competent professional advice, diagnosis or therapy. If expert assistance or counseling is needed, services of a competent professional should be sought. The content of this book (including any techniques or practices) is intended to be used as an adjunct to a rational and responsible healthcare program prescribed by a healthcare practitioner and also is intended to be used only in safe and comfortable circumstances. The Authors and Publisher shall have neither liability nor responsibility to any person or entity with respect to any loss or damage caused or alleged to be caused directly or indirectly by any content, techniques and/or practices or by any error or omission herein. Any perceived slight of specific people or organizations is unintentional. As well as obtaining written or

Kuan Yin Buddhism

oral permissions, all case history names and/or identities have been altered to protect their anonymity. This disclaimer applies to all content, publications, editions, modifications and articles (in all formats) featuring Hope Bradford Cht's content and commentary. Kuan Yin quotes are from the books: <u>Oracle of Compassion: the Living Word of Kuan Yin</u> http://tinyurl.com/yyf2my35 and <u>Kuan Yin: 200+ Timeless Truths</u>

Kuan Yin Buddhism

Table of Contents

Preface

Section One: The Kuan Yin Parables

Section Two: The Kuan Yin Visitations

Section Three: The Kuan Yin Teachings

About Hope Bradford CHt.

Kuan Yin Buddhism

"Sit with me in divine faith and believe in me. And I will be there!...I am energy manifested into form. I don't have any need for material things. Nor, do the laws of karma bind me. I'm free, without any karmic restraints. I don't get a reward for providing you with this information. Instead, I delight in helping to liberate souls. I come from a realm where there is instant, mind to mind understanding. There can be no lies; no misunderstanding. I'm a power magnet. I'll open the hole and what you need for your life will pour into you...When people acknowledge my presence, that's what makes it work. However, I will never force my memory on people. It's all a matter of Free Will. Free Will is very important. People must have Free Will to exist." ~ Kuan Yin

Kuan Yin Buddhism

In China and other parts of the Eastern Hemisphere, accounts of villagers having been visited by Goddess of Compassion and Mercy, Kuan Yin, have been handed down through the ages. While uncommon in the United States and the Western Hemisphere in general, such visitations are not completely unheard of. Along with Kuan Yin's profound parables and spiritual teachings, this manuscript chronicles the deity's numerous visitations to author Hope Bradford following her transcribing of the book: <u>Oracle of Compassion: the Living Word of Kuan Yin</u>. Thus, the receiving of Kuan Yin's spiritual wisdom continues to this very day!

Kuan Yin Buddhism

Preface

"People want to know why I chose Lena and Hope to bring forth my message of loving-kindness to the world. It's alchemy! Lena and Hope's combined energy creates an open channel that I can manifest through. It is very rare in the world. It doesn't matter what nationality a person is. I can go wherever I want. I come to them because they are receptive!" ~ *Kuan Yin*

Humanity has, through the channeled information of extremely intuitive beings, periodically attracted crucial information to assist in understanding the nature of personal and mass reality—that we are eternal beings living a human existence. Throughout, Kuan Yin loosens the Gordian knot of our entanglement within reality. This information is critical as it could prevent repeated incarnations into limiting realities of our own karmic making.

Kuan Yin Buddhism

Reminding Her devotees that there is no beginning or end; only the universal teachings that have eternally been with us, Kuan Yin proclaims: *"Learn from the Elders, those Speakers who came before me. Come to know the basic universal principles. Be open to new learning opportunities."*

Indeed, this transcription of Kuan Yin's profound teachings may have had its origin when Ms. Lees prayed to a beautiful stone visage of the deity. Having traveled from California to visit with family and friends in Philadelphia, Lena knew this would be the last time, for a while, that she'd be able to visit the East Coast. Placing a visit to the University of Pennsylvania Museum of Archaeology and Anthropology on her family's vacation itinerary, Lena had no idea of the importance of her decision, how it would later profoundly transform her life.

At the museum with her husband and children by her side, she suddenly gravitated to a room boasting an impressive display of Asian shrines and statuary. Drawn to a particularly

Kuan Yin Buddhism

striking sculpture of Kuan Yin, Lena believed the statue was comforting her, speaking to her. Beseeching Kuan Yin, she and her family asked for assistance with the many challenges they faced ahead. Several years later; making an appointment with me, Lena found herself engaged in an ongoing conversation; channeling the words and spiritual canons of the ancient Asian deity.

To my amazement, I heard Lena speak, while in trance, powerful phrases and metaphor that were utterly foreign to her. Incredibly, upon waking from her trance, she remembered nothing.

While previously having heard Kuan Yin's name referenced in casual conversation, I was, at this point in my life, nevertheless unfamiliar with the iconography of this Buddhist deity. Believing Lena's first encounter with this Chinese Goddess of Compassion and Mercy was a chance one-time event, I listened attentively (but with a healthy skepticism) during our second session together. By the third episode, I knew that something

Kuan Yin Buddhism

remarkable had occurred. From her first hypnosis induction, forward, Lena realized she had a personal "channel"; some mysterious and lingering connection with Kuan Yin.

From the onset, it appeared Lena had a natural affinity with the Goddess. Further into this channeling phenomenon, it was revealed that Lena had worshiped Kuan Yin throughout many lifetimes, that because of their former relationship Lena's personage was imminently compatible for bearing this Goddess's compassionate message.

When transcribing the Kuan Yin material, I often wondered if this deity somehow knew Lena would always ask selfless questions; that because of her love for humanity, Lena also had true compassion. Indeed, to facilitate an authentic channeling of Kuan Yin's Law of Compassion theories, the once separate consciousnesses of Lena and Kuan Yin were inextricably bound during each of the trance sessions. Typically, Lena's trance discourse (along with masterfully interpreting Kuan Yin's unique language and ever-transforming visages)

Kuan Yin Buddhism

involved questions spontaneously rising up into her consciousness.

Sometimes her inquiries methodically followed the original theme of a given session. On other occasions, however, Lena's new line of questioning could initiate entire new discussion threads. Obviously, new topics spontaneously introduced by Lena were (because of this unique melding of consciousness), at least partially, influenced by Kuan Yin.

Kuan Yin's unique language styling and vast spiritual lexicon is a form of non-linear language. (In many world traditions, there exist classic variations on non-linear language including shamanic journeys and speaking in tongues.) Lena was confronted (at the onset of each discourse) with the challenge of navigating the sometimes-foreboding waters of out-of-time reality. In addition to deciphering Kuan Yin's non-linear verbiage, Lena (as Kuan Yin's spokesperson) would, on occasion, describe the Deity's complex and rapidly-morphing visages.

Also known as Avalokiteshvara, Padmapani, Chenrigzi, Shadakshari, Water,

Kuan Yin Buddhism

Moon Goddess, and Deity with a Thousand Eyes, Kuan Yin has been worshiped at temples, pagodas and shrines throughout the world as both a male and female deity. As this deity came to Ms. Lees as primarily female, I began referring to Kuan Yin (throughout the text), as feminine in nature:

"Now, I see a young woman coming forth from the bamboo clearing. Standing near a waterfall, she is wearing a long flowing robe. Perhaps my eyes deceive me. Maybe it is the sunlight, which makes her appear so radiant! She looks so young. Sweet smile, raven hair swept back; she lovingly returns my stare. Touching the incredible fabric of Her gown, I'm aware of its luxurious softness. It is like touching a thousand feathers. My eyes follow the long trail of her gown as it descends into a black and starry universe. Desperately clasping the gown, as if it were the edge of a cliff, I notice my body is now cradled, supported by it." ~ Lena Lees

Worshiped throughout India (as the male god Avalokitesvara), Japan (as Kannon) and mainland Asia, Kuan Yin has many names

Kuan Yin Buddhism

having many translations, for example: "She who harkens to the cries of the world" or "the Lord who looks upon the world with compassion". Reverence for Kuan Yin is estimated, by many, to date back to Mother Goddess Devi and the Indus Valley Civilization (3000-1500 BC).

    Ancient Indian, Tibetan and Chinese civilizations are therefore considered to be profoundly influenced by Kuan Yin who is known to periodically appear to those who pray to Her for assistance. It is said that She especially makes Her presence known during historical times of great challenge. Indeed, there have been, throughout the millennia, historical accounts of visions of this deity and the wisdom thereby imparted.

    Visiting temples, shrines and pagodas throughout the East, one can bask in the deity's essence, viewing its many forms (for this deity has been described as both male and female—having at least thirty-three transformations) as both sculpture and temple paintings. When viewing these magnificent artifacts, it can be helpful to understand, as spoken in Kuan Yin's own words, Her spiritual evolution:

"I come to each person in a different form. Sometimes, I will come even in the crudest of forms if it leads someone to their rightful path. I provide whatever one's soul wants; whatever one is ready for or evolved to. It's very difficult to keep certain beings on this planet. For those who've come from the higher planes; having had access to other, more heightened senses, experiences here can make the earth feel like a prison."

Discovering, from the Kuan Yin channeling's, that the earth is in a particular "karmic cycle", Lena wanted to understand this deity's perspective on the nature of our present historical era. Lena also had many questions concerning the nature of one's personal path of liberation. This often triggered long and intricate exchanges about how we as citizens of the earth can better comprehend, appreciate and improve upon that which has thus far been manifested.

Kuan Yin Buddhism

During Kuan Yin's deeply spiritual and thought-provoking dialogue, the deity explained: *"It is difficult for some to hear the voices of the Divine Spirit"*. Realizing her rare ability to accurately relay Kuan Yin's complex phrases and concepts had stemmed from her previous worship of the goddess as well as her close connection with me—that together we formed an energy conducive to receiving the Kuan Yin wisdom, Lena continued channeling the profound Kuan Yin Buddhist precepts.

Insistent in Her desire to expand Her spiritual influence, Kuan Yin had implored: *"Make me more real so that I can remind people that I exist. When there are thought processes that invalidate me; when people don't believe I exist, it causes my Presence in the world to be dissipated. When people don't believe in certain things, these things will cease to exist. People are so focused on surviving that they often don't think of me. It's hard for them to remember. When people connect with me and bring me more alive, I can help them. When they acknowledge my presence, that's what makes it work.*

However, I will never force my memory on people. It's all a matter of Free Will. Free Will is very important. People have to have Free Will to exist."

She then revealed those geographical areas on earth where Her essence is most pronounced:

"There are places where one can feel closer to and rejuvenate one's spirit. While some have acquired many material things, they've perhaps lost something in the area of spirituality. Geographically, China is a place that holds elements of my energy. Don't only take into consideration the government [when determining the spiritual significance of a particular region]. It can be regarded as a thin, paper veil, indeed a 'front-drop' for a greater energy. Mexico is another geographical location possessing a similar energy to mine." ~ Kuan Yin

Kuan Yin's primary messages are that we do indeed create/attract reality, we are here to learn compassion and Her "Love and Forgiveness Principle" and we are eternal

Kuan Yin Buddhism

beings. Indeed, Buddha has said: *"All that we are is the result of what we have thought: it is founded on our thoughts, it is made up of our thoughts. If a man speaks or acts with a pure thought, happiness follows him, like a shadow that never leaves him".*

A spiritualist and hypnotherapist, I've been profoundly influenced since witnessing and transcribing the Kuan Yin Buddhist parables as revealed in the book: <u>Oracle of Compassion: the Living Word of Kuan Yin</u>. It was during that time that Kuan Yin promised to appear again to me—that we enjoyed a very personal relationship. Included in this latest work, <u>Kuan Yin Buddhism: The Kuan Yin Parables, Visitations and Teachings</u>, I will delineates my amazing dreams and experiences with this revered deity of the Chinese Pantheon—that in addition to the originally-set down teachings, the ancient wisdom continues to this very day!

Divided into three main sections: The Kuan Yin Parables, Visitations and Teachings, this manuscript defines not only Kuan Yin's main

Kuan Yin Buddhism

Buddhist principles, but also demonstrates how each uniquely wonderful person can daily benefit from Her teachings.

The Kuan Yin Buddhism teachings presented herein can help you understand: *Your purpose in life *The Love and Forgiveness Principle *How the moment is one's link to eternity *The power of sound and vibration *The power of imagination *Reincarnation *Love and relationships

Kuan Yin Buddhism

Kuan Yin Buddhism

Section One: The Kuan Yin Parables

Herein, deity of compassion and mercy, Kuan Yin, provides Her modern timeless truths; a moral template for humanity to proceed forth from. Speaking through psychic channel Lena Lees, Kuan Yin explained why Her contemporary spiritual parables and teachings (while having certain similarities to other traditional spiritual paths) may differ from those of ancient times:

"Tradition is good. However, in the Western Culture there are so many people searching for wisdom. It is important to get familiar with the various paths. Such a process develops character for one to look inward for their right path...It's an urgent time for energies to evolve...The process is being sped up, an acceleration creating awe-inspiring changes affecting every aspect of life. There are a group of souls who are using this time to help propel them forward. This process can be compared to a ship catching the wind in a certain way. Those

catching this wind will need to be skillful. And like a sailor's knowledge and deep respect for the sea, these people will need to know when to turn the ship and when to let go. Adept in utilizing the winds of these times, they will have me as their sail...Your precious earth cannot be destroyed. Sometimes it just looks that way." ~ Kuan Yin

Skillfully utilizing the art of parable, Kuan Yin's stunningly beautiful and powerful storytelling, backdrops and shape-shifts clarify Her precepts such as the everlasting legitimacy of the soul—that beneath ego's perfunctory mask is the ubiquitous All-That-Is. The individual, as part of the Infinite Spectrum of Existence, thus possesses Free Will to change their personal karma (objects and events manifested in one's waking reality) through changing their beliefs.

Throughout history, mystics have taught that we've incarnated on this plane of existence for the express purpose of learning to manipulate matter—that admittance to the advanced realms requires that such a skill first be mastered: *"Remember the mystics of each religion. In any religion, you'll find the truth if you study the mystics. The profound answers are found in mysticism." ~ Kuan Yin.* Surely, therefore, those in the higher realms will attempt to communicate such teachings to those who are receptive.

Indeed, souls incarnate to earth aware of the contrast; the blend of events and consciousnesses they'll be immersed in—knowing that this discord is the catalyst pushing them to redefine their personal manifestation-skills. All the while, each individual holds, within their inner being, the memory of the higher consciousness realms serving as the axiom for all cultural morals and comparisons. The bulwark of the Kuan Yin parables, these universal truths demonstrates consciousness's profound flexibility in the creation of personal reality:

"There's a beautiful tree where I used to go when I was a teenager," describes Lena. *"It stands majestic, atop the rolling hills behind the house where I grew up. When I was lonely and*

Kuan Yin Buddhism

sad about my life, I used to go there. Kuan Yin is at the tree looking very luminous. I see the bark of the tree, which looks very real, very three-dimensional. For some reason, Kuan Yin is touching the trunk of the tree. Suddenly, She seems very small next to me and she wants me to touch the tree. I'm not sure why. There is a tiny bird, with pretty feathers in its nest. It is about the size of a wren. I see the texture of the tree. I think it might be a birch. I'm not sure. 'Why should I touch the tree,' I ask. She's telling me that I created the tree, that it is another realm I was able to visit when life was too painful and lonely at home."

"You created the tree! You create your whole world with thoughts," assures Kuan Yin.

"Everyone creates realities based on their own personal beliefs. It is very complicated to hold the dream and live the dream. You are learning the art of juggling the dream and the world of dreams!"

Integral to this process, one must necessarily develop a specific kind of focus. Such ability is required for identifying the

Kuan Yin Buddhism

shape and breadth of one's thought and emotion formations. Having their unique and indelible residues, visions combined with thoughts and emotions create the blueprint for personal reality. Intimately associated with molecular process theories, the building up and breaking down of these imprints create uncountable parallel universes.

Demonstrated by the following Kuan Yin parable and emphasized throughout the Kuan Yin session's, was the deity's insistence that as multidimensional beings living an earthly existence, we are indestructible!

"*'I see Kuan Yin today,'* describes Lena from her trance. *'She is glowing; radiating forth so many beautiful colors. She's showing me a lotus root in the mud; how something so beautiful can survive, indeed thrive, in the messy mud. She's telling me that this is the human condition; that human evolution from the 'mud' inevitably creates a beautiful outcome. She is more beautiful than I've ever seen Her.*

Wearing a gold kimono adorned with dazzling necklaces and bracelets, Kuan Yin is

Kuan Yin Buddhism

now riding a dragon. Below the ominous, stormy clouds, the sea now churns; its once calm waters whipped into a frenzy by the wind gusting at hurricane speed. Presenting me with a beautiful Carp, Kuan Yin is calm, happy inside the maelstrom. I hear Her say, 'Here is a beautiful Carp that I'm giving to you!'

Now, the sea is even stormier than before. Kuan Yin is undulating; changing into another form. In the past, I've described this process as shape-shifting. I realize, however, that Kuan Yin's transformations involve a change in Her molecular makeup—that She progresses from being physical to a formation similar to ectoplasm.

For a moment, I see a beautiful white bird. Once again, though, Kuan Yin is back in Her original form, wearing the gold-colored kimono. Today, I notice the many varied Kuan Yin transformations. Earlier in the session, She wanted to demonstrate something. Her form suddenly got very hot and then ignited into a white/blue fireball. Emerging from that experience, She became whole once again. Nothing can harm Her!

I suddenly see Kuan Yin as the male form, Avalokitesvara. Assuming His relaxed pose, with one knee up. Kuan Yin then takes the shape of Her female form. Her jet-black hair gracefully flowing down over the back of her white, silk kimono, Kuan Yin is just there, waiting in the storm when an immense hole opens above Her.

Emerging from the opening are scientists, mathematicians, composers, artists, etc. They seem very frustrated as they want to help with the recovery of the earth. When living on earth they were very attached to their work and became quite famous. They are suspended in their parallel world, just waiting for a pathway to open through the Maya, so they can once again assist the earth. I hear them say: "There's a current! We can't connect to someone unless they're on a spiritual path. Maya is incredibly difficult to penetrate through! There are historically notable people forced to wait on the other side until they can ride this current—this pathway and help the earth. Now," *reveals*

Kuan Yin Buddhism

Lena, *"I'm seeing Thousand Arms Kuan Yin. She's saying, 'I can help you in many ways with many outcomes!'"*

Showing the complex nature of existence—that we are eternal, multidimensional beings living an earthly existence, the above parable also demonstrates the power of remaining calm in the midst of a storm. It is this *Kuan Yin Spirit* that the deity would like us to practice: *"You're the Watcher. Instead of judging, you just see!"*

Revealing that spirit energies want to connect with those living on earth, the above parable is similar to the following metaphorical example showing humans as eternal beings who can never be destroyed:

"I don't really know what I'm seeing. I just see many shapes and forms of Kuan Yin," continues Lena. *"Now I'm witnessing a scene of Hiroshima, a great mushroom cloud. She's inside it. Now it is inside of her. Suddenly, it explodes in her body and she absorbs, becomes the energy. That's her message for this chapter. Nothing can harm Her. Even the most*

devastating force is changed, softened so that people will grow even when experiencing complete destruction. She's not afraid to merge with the most fearsome creations."

"*You see,*" announces Kuan Yin, "*I am still in my original form. It didn't destroy me.*"

In another session, Kuan Yin demonstrated how sound and music can help one stay calm in the midst of chaos:

"*I'm here in the bamboo garden,*" explained Lena. "*Kuan Yin is very illuminated. Her garment is so bright, so filled with light. She's holding a musical instrument. I think it is a lute. Completely focused upon tuning this instrument—trying to get the sound just right, she does not speak.*"

"*Sit down, Lena, and see what I'm doing,*" instructed Kuan Yin. "*Once this instrument is correctly tuned and kept tuned, any amount of chaos won't matter, won't influence it.*"

"*Of course,*" maintains Lena, "*this is Kuan Yin's metaphor for keeping the body chakras well-tuned. She's telling me this is a continuation of her message concerning the effects of sound and vibrations upon physicality. She is also saying that the power of sound (and pulse) is why music is so calming and comforting."*

Exquisitely-demonstrated in the Deity's next parable, was Kuan Yin's teaching on allowing events to naturally unfold through savoring the present moment. Rather than always pushing towards a given goal, allow for the magnetizing of what you want to achieve through the power of the Law of Attraction:

Upon being counted down from fifteen to zero to her trance state, Lena immediately began laughing in delight:

"I didn't expect Kuan Yin to show up so soon. It's extraordinary! She's perched on top of an elephant:

"I had to come in a different form today, to shake you; to get you out of a certain expectation of me."

"She wants me to come along. So I guess I'll just come along; riding on top of this huge elephant. I'm just wondering how I will be able to climb on."

"Don't think like an earthling! Don't analyze every step. Just get on."

"It's kind of a nice sensation. The elephant's body is swaying heavily but gently. I feel its power and yet at the same time there is a softness and consistency to the elephant's gait. Even though this kind of travel is slow and rocking, I'm still getting somewhere. It is a sensation that is at once soothing and yet forceful."

"See how I don't have to try too hard. The elephant effortlessly carries me (us) on her back."

Silently pondering Kuan Yin's potent communication Lena stops speaking for a moment.

"There is something Kuan Yin is trying to show to me about love, compassion and power," comments Lena, from the depths of her trance. *"That just experiencing the power of the elephant moving along is important. Kuan Yin is also telling me to listen to the sounds of the jungle, to just be with what is.*

Kuan Yin Buddhism

'But Kuan Yin,' I now ask, 'How do I know when to push or to just sit and be with something?'

I'm going to be silent for a moment and listen to Kuan Yin's answer. I'm getting the impression that Kuan Yin is trying to show me how to be aware of the signals. When I mentioned to you, Hope, that I was going to listen for Kuan Yin's answer, I noticed at that very moment, the elephant had turned; rambling towards a small lake."

"The elephant needs a drink of water," Kuan Yin explained in a matter-of-fact way. "So she temporarily veered off the path, traveling to the lake. When she's satisfied she'll return to the original path. The elephant's 'break' then, is good for everyone involved, helping them to better get along."

"We've now returned to the trail. Kuan Yin seems to know where we're headed. She has a stick in her hand."

"It's a directional tool. I would never hurt anything. Instead, I just touch one or the other flank, to instruct the elephant which way I want *to go. One can't just 'hit life' and expect it will cooperate; go the way one wants. Maybe it will and maybe it won't. You might have heard the sayings, 'the path is the goal' or 'the journey is the goal'. These sayings are often antithetical to the reality of living in your culture. Your culture is very "goal structured". There is frequently a push to be "where one is supposed to be" rather than savoring where one is right now,"* observes Kuan Yin.

This is cultural, not instinctual. Naturally, one needs a driving force to survive. However, the concept of having specific goals is very Western. This kind of mindset makes people very ambitious. However, no one is obligated to live his life by this Western view of things.

It is important to have an idea of the path one wants to be on. This statement comes with the warning that one not be too attached to the outcome. To have a concept about the nature of one's life path can be a skillful tool in living one's life. However, there is a danger that one will misconstrue a goal to be the entire purpose of one's life and in so doing perhaps create a negative driving force. Don't be too harsh on yourself concerning the choices you've made during your life. When one subtracts from the equation of life physical birth and death, one can regard lessons learned as forming an infinite line.

Then one can say, 'I'm learning this right now'. Try to crystallize the components of the lesson, excluding as much as is possible gender and financial factors. Repeat to yourself: 'this is the lesson I'm learning right now, at this exact moment in time'."

The elephant is a metaphor for the original vehicle; the driving force for one's life path. It decides and then you decide."

"The elephant's behavior is suddenly becoming very erratic," Lena exclaims, somewhat nervously. *"I can't control her direction. She's going every which way."*

"Riding upon a female elephant in heat is not so good," acknowledges Kuan Yin. *"We can no longer make her our ride down the path. It's not fair to the elephant. We're going to have to trade her in for another elephant or walk."*

"We've jumped off the elephant and now we're walking," Lena conveys.

"If you don't have transportation and you want to stay on the path, you'll just have to walk," advises Kuan Yin.

"When one feels pulled to do a particular thing, when one has passion for a certain life path, the deepest aspect of oneself is always involved. In such an instance, (if the goal is worthy and makes one happy), one should continue on that same life path.

Just because the elephant can't carry you anymore doesn't mean you should give up your goal. Continue down the path that makes you feel fulfilled. Those who continue on an unrewarding path for the sake of only monetary gain are displaying a lack of trust in life. Continuing in such a mistrustful way could bring impoverishment. Following one's heart, continuing on one's divine path can bring abundance."

Your beliefs and how you regard yourself form the living-root creating your personal pathway. Likening the elephant to one's innate,

Kuan Yin Buddhism

intuitive *driving force*; insisting: *"It decides and then you decide"*, Kuan Yin is decidedly cautious towards the "Western" notion of always pushing oneself to a greater limit.

Furthermore, She declares that it is these intuitive, emotional impulses welling from deep within that should form the guiding; indeed *driving,* force for one's life pathway. Carefully listening to this inner Source can align you with your unique Path of Liberation; thereby attracting your birthright of health, wealth and happiness!

Because they are universal, Kuan Yin's parables and teachings apply no matter what paradigm humans have created: *"You must acknowledge and experience this part of the universe. Earth is a place to live out karma. There are other places, other possibilities. Don't get too dragged down where the karma is thick. Concentrate on creating the possibilities. There are endless possibilities to build your story around. Refrain from building your story on only one way of thinking. Open up your psyches!*

Kuan Yin Buddhism

Refrain from worrying or thinking there is only one possibility or one solution." ~ Kuan Yin

Confirming that our life here on earth is an opportunity for us to fully realize the power of the moment, the Kuan Yin parables shows that the time linearity of earth offers a unique window of opportunity for achieving lasting fulfillment. Focusing upon the powerful dynamics of Universal Law, Kuan Yin Buddhism demonstrates that earth is a realm designed for transformation and empowerment: *"There really are demigods waiting in line to be born, to manifest as humans. In this way, they can evolve faster. It is so, then, that everyone comes to earth to further evolve."~ Kuan Yin*

Kuan Yin's spiritual parables and teachings address how we can resolve many dilemmas threatening modern mankind through fully understanding and developing our humanity. In our physical, social and spiritual lives, we need to discover the optimum balance. Giving form and direction to our lives, these universal teachings can bring to the fore pre-existing extraordinary potentials that we may have largely ignored:

"Yes, through your thoughts, beliefs and emotions, you create your reality. Knowing this voids any supposed debt from other lifetimes. I know it is sometimes difficult to differentiate between free will and karma. Focus upon your free will and your ability to create reality. I'm optimistic and hopeful you can do this."

Quite apart from arriving at her usual sacred place with the bamboo forest and waterfall backdrop during trance, Lena once found herself standing on a shoreline somewhere in the Eastern hemisphere of the world, perhaps in Eastern China:

"I'm standing on a beach. Everything seems so real. I'm not seeing a lot of sand. Instead, I notice profoundly beautiful round stones stretching as far as the eye can see. Kuan Yin is here. She is like Venus, statuesque and standing in front of a beautiful pink half-shell. Quickly, she walks in front of me, pointing the way.

Kuan Yin Buddhism

We are entering the mouth of a cave. It's so interesting. I see stairs carved out of rock in the cave. We walk up the stairs to a door. I know somehow this is just another entrance, a doorway to another time, place. Perhaps at another historical time monks lived there. Now, I'm seeing a huge image; a beautiful statue of Kuan Yin at the very top of the mountain. There are stairs leading up to her. It is as if I'm right on location, standing alongside a group of worshippers.

I feel the potency of Kuan Yin's energy. In these places, perhaps China or Vietnam, there is a palpable sense of being immersed in and supported by her presence. There is a need by the people to know more, to pick up and accumulate wisdom.

I'm suddenly feeling a need to be in that kind of energy. However, it's not an intellectual kind of need. It's a bit different from the more male-impacted Buddhism."

Lena then hears Kuan Yin speak:

"Some believe I am in servitude to Buddha. However, Buddha doesn't see it that

Kuan Yin Buddhism

way. We're more like brother and sister. I'm showing, Lena, my abode, a place on earth where humans can visit me and be in my potency. Lena is looking at my statue and then at my form. There's a difference. I come to people in many forms, forms constructed from people's own perceptions of how I should come to them. And it is individual spiritual needs that create these unique perceptions. In the end, it does not matter what form I take."

Insisting that Her love and forgiveness mindset is *"the most powerful force in the universe"*, Kuan Yin explained that magnification of such a force could change the entire earth consciousness: *"If enough people knew about this, if every human being could recognize the power of the Love and Forgiveness Principle all consciousness on earth would change instantly. Indeed, thoughts can change the course of history. Sometimes, all it takes is enough people knowing a certain concept."*

Additionally, according to Kuan Yin, our earthly existence is the most important step in our evolution where we, as limitless, spiritual

Kuan Yin Buddhism

beings, achieve physical manifestation in all of its complexities; wherein beliefs, intentions and desires are the driving forces for the personal creation of reality.

A main significance of the goddess's imaginative transformations is that they are metaphors for the personal transformation of thought into matter. Her following *windsurfer parable* emphasizes the importance of focusing on only that which you want to achieve—how proper Focused Intent can help one successfully "ride" (manipulate) one's present reality:

"You can have a hope. However, to agonize over the future is not very skillful," Kuan Yin relays.

"Kuan Yin is showing me picture of a windsurfer skimming effortlessly along the ocean's surface," describes Lena.

"While quite skilled, he is nevertheless very focused on the elements around him. The windsurfer is focused upon how to turn the sail. His question must always be, 'what am I going

to do with the wind that is blowing right now,'" instructs Kuan Yin.

"There are the waves and there is the wind, seen and unseen forces. Everyone has these same elements in their lives, the seen and unseen: karma and free will. The question is, 'How are you going to handle what you have?' You are riding the karmic wave underneath and the wind can shift. Everyone must take what they see and deal with that which is unseen. Fall into the water!"

Emerging from the mists of Lena Lees' trance-epiphany, transforming into myriad manifestations of the original Oneness, Kuan Yin's shape-shifts are emblematic of Her timeless truths; heralding the deity's triumphant return. Insisting that it is for each of us to fathom the mystery of Her parables and myriad visages, Kuan Yin reveals (with every nuance) humanity's manifestation powers. Becoming one with the surroundings, this deity weaves the intimate fabric: our inextricable enmeshment with nature and the universe:

Kuan Yin Buddhism

"I see a beautiful burgundy-colored teardrop-shaped gem with many facets," reveals Lena. *"I can see that cushions have been placed in a circle around the entire interior of the gem. I sense it is a very happy place. Someone is sending me inside of the gem through one of the facets that has now opened. My acceptance into this new world is to show me that I am a gem in God's eyes, that we are all gems in God's eyes. We are perfect and eternally valuable just as we are. The door I am led through is actually one of the facets of the gem. I didn't expect that I would be able to go there. I feel as if I'm a genie in a bottle. It's almost comical that I'm in the gem.*

Now, I notice how when Kuan Yin sits in Her traditional pose, She is the same teardrop shape as the gem. In Her pale green robe, She looks so beautiful as She sits facing me. In her hands, She holds her body of healing elixir. I'm suddenly aware that I've been placed inside the gem as a reminder of how precious I am and how precious every living entity is. I hear Kuan Yin say: 'You are the gem. I want you to experience being inside this very precious gem.'

Kuan Yin Buddhism

I now understand that this gem is so precious that no one, not a millionaire, not even a billionaire could afford it. Suddenly I hear Kuan Yin again say, 'You're like this gem.'"

"Yes, you're like a precious gem to so many people," I'd reiterated.

Seeing that Lena needs a glass of water, I got up from my chair to go to the kitchen.

"Kuan Yin doesn't want you to go. Please don't move," exclaimed Lena. "Hope, I need you to continue sitting close to me. If you get up from the chair you could break the connection. Remember? You are the conduit for Her teachings!"

Kuan Yin continues: *"My beautiful Hope! How I love you! Each person is also the gem. Everyone is suffering because they've forgotten who they are; that they are also this precious gem. It's so sad to see people suffer because they've forgotten who they are."*

"Kuan Yin wants people to (whenever they don't feel valuable), to meditate on the burgundy gem. Kuan Yin is wearing a necklace with the burgundy gem," explains Lena.

Kuan Yin Buddhism

Then Kuan Yin states: *"I wear it around my neck to remind people that they are actually gems and that they can meditate upon it to know this. That's why God created me. If I'm called, I'll go to that person and give them compassion.*

Nothing anyone can do, no matter how detestable, can take away my compassion for them. Life is all about compassion; compassion for yourself and others. I'm in this world during this Kali Yuga era—this time of great turmoil, to help people learn compassion. Events keep happening to make the people's compassion greater." ~ Kuan Yin

Compassion at the level personified by Kuan Yin is not some luxury sentiment that might be expressed towards others at the appropriate moment. Indeed, it is at the very core of humanity's survival. And as Kuan Yin's Law of Compassion is intimately connected with all daily choices and emotions, such compassionate feelings on the part of the ego will join and expand the great rhapsody of light

Kuan Yin Buddhism

and sound stretching beyond any time/space constraints.

In this final example of the Kuan Yin Parables, the deity explains the power of beliefs and Focused Intent in the creation of reality:

"Kuan Yin is changing back to her pastime of riding a dragon on the ocean. In her right hand, she holds a globe. In her left hand she carries a staff. I'm not sure what the globe represents. Now I'm here with her. She is beautiful, maybe around forty-five years old. She is sitting in her traditional position. I notice how the folds of her robe seem to be much more than cloth. They seem to hold a mysterious energy. Now, she is pouring us some tea, Hope. Seated upon a beautiful piece of cloth, together, we're near a beautiful waterfall."

"Just be with me, now," entices Kuan Yin. *"We can sip tea and be together."*

"This is really nice!" replies Lena to Kuan Yin.

Then, addressing me, Lena relays: *"What is wonderful about this whole experience is that Kuan Yin is completely present. She's not just here with me. She's in my heart quadrant. She's in me. She has an astonishing ability to be present.*

I'm seeing how one's mind can distract, can come between one another. Here and now (with Kuan Yin), there is no space between our complete focused attentions. The energy is unbroken, continuous. It's like a meditation. Even as she is pouring tea, I feel a thread, a connection—the real possibility that she can be carried within us, me. I'm going to drink the tea in honor of her presence. Kuan Yin is telling me: 'You, Hope, can drink it too!'"

"She's going to take me on a journey. I look into the cup of tea and am suddenly going into the universe. I'm trailing on her robes. However, they're not really robes. There is something important about her clothing, her flowing garments. She can use them to demonstrate, to create like a canvas. Kuan Yin is saying: "I knew Hope would understand that. The folds of the material can become any reality, for example, landscapes, other universes!"

Kuan Yin Buddhism

Now, we are flying in the universe," continues Lena. *"However, at the same time we seem to be flying over America. Miles and miles of farmland! This time, instead of taking me to Iraq, Kuan Yin is taking me to what appears to be the state of Texas. Kuan Yin informs me that today we are focusing on petroleum and what it represents: money and power!*

She is saying that the energy of certain oil families (including the parents and grandparents) can also include anyone in or out of body attracted to them. There is an intense need for money. I can feel it. It is almost as if they're suffocating and the oil helps them to breathe," marvels Lena. *"There are the [aforementioned] families as well as their ancestral legacies to oil:*

"They need the oil because it is like oxygen for them,'" reveals Kuan Yin. "There are some beings that need particular elements. You know how a physician may prescribe specific vitamins or minerals for a patient? The Vedas often recommend certain stones, gems or

Kuan Yin Buddhism

crystals be carried for one's protection or general well being.

Some energies require the element of oil to breathe, (whether metaphorical or not). And, of course, breath is life. Certain individuals need these elements. Over time, misguided forces; disembodied spirit energies (souls) hovering over the earth, have created these particular families.

Everyone creates (expansive or limiting) realities based on their own personal beliefs. However, some beliefs are so powerful as to potentially create limiting realities over and over. There is now so much global investment in the belief that oil is life. The energy has been built up to such an extent as to attract similar out-of-body spirits. Someone who is actually quite weak can appear strong when 'backed' by these spirits.

Indeed, behind the above oil families is a powerful mass of souls who believe strongly that oil is life. They also have the mindset that it is the only thing keeping them in existence. In other words, if the belief goes, so do they.

Kuan Yin Buddhism

So, this inaccurate belief system, this 'untruth' has magnified itself. And as in all inaccurate belief systems, nature will oppose it because it is too dense,' decrees Kuan Yin. *'Conversely, Nirvana is very light, very ethereal. Untruth must be broken down into no thought. This untruth will come up against a great opposition."*

Continuing to describe the disk, Lena states, *"It is very hard in texture. Kuan Yin is lifting it up like a mountain. It's like a giant disk of great density. She's balancing it on her staff while continuing to ride upon the dragon across the ocean. Nevertheless, she still maintains a sense of hope.*

I ask Kuan Yin how she will dissolve this hard mass constructed of the limiting belief systems [the "not enough", "better than" and "survival of the fittest" beliefs]. She tells me the energy of "good" will reach the souls like a prayer. Kuan Yin is also telling me the disk cannot just be destroyed. If that strategy is ever attempted, many will perish. I'm confused," confesses Lena. *"Certainly, I don't want anyone* to die. What's to be done with it; this strange and dense energy?"

"What do you think we can do with it, Lena?" Kuan Yin casts this crucial question back to Lena.

Just then, my pen ran dry. Why was this happening at such a critical time? Was it destiny? Not having the luxury to continue my pondering, I knew more pens were in the cabinet at the other end of the living room. Leaping up, I awkwardly blurt out: *"Wait just a moment, Lena. I'm out of ink. I just need to go get another pen!"*

"I just understood it!" exclaims Lena. *"Just when you jumped up to get another pen, Hope, I finally understood what Kuan Yin is trying to tell me. Kuan Yin says everything being spoken and written about the Iraq War is shedding light on this limiting belief system, slowly dissolving the disk. Each of us will help to break it down slowly. And people will evolve to understand it,"* concludes Lena, with a sigh of relief.

Kuan Yin Buddhism

"Many people are unaware they buy into this belief system,' notes Kuan Yin. 'Nevertheless, they go on believing the only way they'll survive is to have money. The [above-discussed] oil families represent the majority's relationship with prosperity and survival. Humanity has created itself around the "survival of the fittest" belief and the fearful belief that there are not enough resources.

Unfortunately, many individuals really believe there are not enough resources for everyone. Additionally, the disembodied souls are not aware they don't really need oil to breathe; that they are fabricating situations they believe they need to survive. So many have made an 'agreement', then, that there isn't enough. War and any other dilemma focusing on hate, fear and murder is based on the belief of not enough and the illusion of survival of the fittest."

"I'm feeling as though I'm underwater and unable to breathe," reveals Lena.

"It took a long time for your planet to evolve into this crisis,' continues Kuan Yin. *"We*

are witnessing the greed and bad behavior of certain individuals. It is a very potent time. People are learning. And what they learn also sets them [the above-mentioned individuals] free. They will no longer be trapped in their own belief system. People will begin to get sparks of light. There will increasingly be more and more sparks which will erode the darkness of confusion," Kuan Yin prophesizes.

[Here, Kuan Yin asserts that certain members of the above families can be very "weak energies". According to the Goddess, in such circumstances, more powerful (out-of-body) energies "can therefore work through them; using the earth bodies for their own purposes".]

"Isn't it curious Lena? Think about what drives you in your life and how many of those beliefs are not serving you well. I'm very grateful for our connection, for this opportunity to meet with you."

"Kuan Yin is touching the arm—I mean the shoulder of this belief system. She is putting her

Kuan Yin Buddhism

hand on the 'shoulder' with utmost compassion," describes Lena.

"I'm sorry for your anguish," consoles Kuan Yin, gently.

"I understand now," Lena exclaims softly. *"Many of these energies are not in human form. Kuan Yin is putting her hand on the thoughts that make up the dense disk. Now I truly see what she is doing. It's alchemy!"*

"Yes! There's a balance that makes something holistic and in truth." responds Kuan Yin. "What I am placing my hand upon is a dense conglomeration of stuck energy made up of certain ideas. Naturally, not all ideas are included in this energy. It needs certain elements, things sprinkled into it gradually.

Having compassion for the "untruth", that is what's missing. I'm sending compassion into this rock. One needs to slowly add elements of insight to reach truth. It's a good time to ask ourselves to look at any lies we are telling ourselves. It's a powerful time to examine one's own thoughts and the thoughts of the people of the world.

Kuan Yin Buddhism

Let us all reflect upon the great mix of free will and karma. Reread the past chapters and ponder what I have said. Karma is intricate, detailed. One cannot dwell on only one particle of this great collective energy. Your life is but one frame of an entire reel of film,' instructs Kuan Yin, reiterating concepts from previous sessions.

Everyone has her or his part. Some don't perform any of their part as they have incomplete or incorrect belief systems. Sometimes it seems as if this world is completely chaotic and sometimes it really is. However, there is a corrective force, an actual physical force."

"Kuan Yin is showing me this force," says Lena; describing what she is witnessing: *"It's a pendulum. No. It's more like a spiral. It seems very complicated. I want to understand, to know more about this structure…"*

"You don't need to necessarily understand everything about the forces—the dynamics of the universe. However, you need to have faith that the process is guided and correct, that it is

ultimately good and that there exists a kind of cosmic steering of evolution, a reason for all of this," counsels Kuan Yin. *"It's already finished! The past, present and future have already occurred.*

Events that seem so cruel and unforgivable...Have faith and trust that even these happenings are ultimately an expression of goodness. Certain religions say things are planned; everything is already worked out. In a very real sense, this is so. All the pain and suffering! It's like a dream. It doesn't go on forever. The suffering does end."

"I want to ask Kuan Yin something," Lena begins to speak.

"Lena, you need to develop your faith and your trust," interrupts Kuan Yin. *"Please try to work on that. Look into your childhood. You came into the world surrounded by violence. Thus, you developed a belief system around fear. Try to remember the universe is on the right course. You no longer have to live life through a veil of fear. You can go beyond it to a place of peace and trust.*

Kuan Yin Buddhism

Now it is time to end the session, for today. It's difficult to let you go. These times together are a way for me to give and communicate my loving compassion. I love when people realize and validate the gifts I send. I'll always be there to comfort and help those in need. I delight in helping others."

"I realize that the tea party is ending," comments Lena. "I touch her hand and say goodbye. I've never known anyone to love me as much as Kuan Yin does. She is still riding the dragon. She is holding the globe and the staff with the dense disk on top of it as She rides away."

In this book delineating the Kuan Yin Buddhism, the deity states: *"I know the whole story. You're at page ten but I understand the entire evolution. In reality, it's already over. It's a dream. Remember? You're living a dream. It's very complicated to hold the dream and live the dream. You are learning the art of juggling the dream and the world of dreams!"*

Kuan Yin Buddhism

Kuan Yin Buddhism

Section Two: The Kuan Yin Visitations

Highly venerated deity in the Chinese Pantheon and known by thousands throughout the ages, Kuan Yin has periodically appeared and spoken to villagers throughout the Orient. Spreading comfort and wisdom, She is the embodiment of mercy and compassion.

Consecrated ground, Kuan Yin's sacred sites are considered Her abodes. Because of their purity, these locations are also designated as Her pilgrimage sites and places of worship.

During the ongoing Kuan Yin trance sessions for the book: <u>Oracle of Compassion: the Living Word of Kuan Yin</u>, there seemed an inexplicable element at work. Although Lena attempted several times to channel Kuan Yin's words without me being present, her extraordinary channeling abilities primarily occurred only when I was in the room with her. During a memorable passage, Kuan Yin mentioned that not only was her energy

Kuan Yin Buddhism

congruent with Lena's energy, but that she also enjoyed a special connection with me.

Lena and I both came to believe the process was more complicated than we'd originally imagined; that my energy somehow served as a psychic fulcrum assisting Lena in bringing forth the Kuan Yin material: *"Kuan Yin sends you a band of energy, Hope. I'm seeing a graphic. It's as if Kuan Yin sends you a band of energy. The band looks almost like the Milky Way, where nebulae are constantly born. It travels through you to me, so that I can speak the Kuan Yin wisdom."*

Often, while Kuan Yin was answering my questions, Lena would observe Kuan Yin moving close and embracing me: *"She's right by you. Kuan Yin has her arms around you, Hope. Kuan Yin wants you to know that she loves and counts on you so much!"*

Well into the writing of: <u>Oracle of Compassion: the Living Word of Kuan Yin</u>, another curious event occurred. Inviting a close friend, Susan, over to see my remodeled dining room, I was delighted to visit with her

Kuan Yin Buddhism

once again. Showing her a Kuan Yin painting I'd just completed, we sat on the couch, having tea and visiting together. It had been a while since we'd seen each other, so there was a lot of catching up to do.

Preparing to leave, Susan pointed excitedly towards the dining-room window, exclaiming: *"Look! Just beyond the window! I see Kuan Yin! She is telling me you're to construct a grotto with a painting of her inside, right out there in the garden."*

Then regarding me intently, Susan asked, *"Are there really such things? I mean stone grottos containing paintings or sculptures of Kuan Yin?"*

"Oh yes," I replied. "They're quite common in the East. There are roadside grottos where people come to worship and pray to the Goddess."

"I know it's really Kuan Yin because I'm seeing Her many arms," relayed Susan, excitedly. *"Can you see? I've got goose bumps! The hair is standing up on my arms. That's how I know this is happening to me; that*

Kuan Yin Buddhism

what I'm witnessing is really true."

Peering in the direction that Susan had been pointing, I replied, *"I know, Her spirit has been a constant presence throughout the creation of this manuscript—encouraging me to continue on throughout the entire process."*

Approaching the time of the actual layout and production of the book, I was haunted by a series of dreams in which a seemingly stranger; a pregnant woman was the main character. Apparently on the verge of giving birth, she came to me nightly for almost a week. While I couldn't be certain, I always suspected this mysterious woman was Kuan Yin, foretelling the completion of <u>Oracle of Compassion: the Living Word of Kuan Yin</u>.

After that, I dreamt of giving birth to a beautiful babe swathed in white silken brocade. Leaving the infant's side for but a moment, I was shocked to discover an empty cradle upon my return. Awakened by my own sheer terror, I realized this dream was but a metaphor; that the challenging, inspirational

Kuan Yin Buddhism

process of chronicling Kuan Yin's message and pastimes was now complete. Moving through like air being breathed in and then out again, the Kuan Yin spiritual teachings could now be released to the world.

Nearing the completion of the Kuan Yin channelings, Kuan Yin had said: *"I'll continue sending Hope important dreams. I have a very personal relationship with her."*

Then, Lena mentioned, *"You know, Hope, how it is quite difficult for me to channel Kuan Yin without you being present?"*

"Yes, we seem to work well together."

"I don't quite understand," pondered Lena. *"Oh I'm seeing how it all works, now. It's alchemy! It's like two wires coming together to create a spark. It's similar to intimate relationships. Kuan Yin is happy with her connection with you Hope!"*

In the months and years following my participation in the completion of <u>Oracle of Compassion: the Living Word of Kuan Yin</u>, I did, in accordance with the deity's former declaration—that she would continue sending

Kuan Yin Buddhism

important dreams, experience many dreams and visitations from Kuan Yin. It was after completing the transcription of some of the Kuan Yin quotes that I fell into a deep slumber. Just before awakening, I dreamt of Kuan Yin standing in my living room directly in front of the marble-tiled fireplace wherein Lena Lees and I would hold prayer circles.

    So real was this vision that I could hear the deity's sweet voice explain that there is a specific meditation for connecting with the Celestial Wisdom! Witnessing Kuan Yin lie face down on the Oriental Carpet with arms outstretched over Her head, I watched as Her thumb and forefinger formed a triangle—the dhyana mudra specifically designated to Kannon called the dhyana mudra displayed by the fourth Dhyani Buddha Amitabha, also known as Amitayus Kuan Yin. It was then that Kuan Yin further explained the significance of this specific mudra; that it acts similar to a capstone on an obelisk—drawing wisdom to one who has demonstrated intention to be a teacher of wisdom.

Aware that Kuan Yin was pointed in a northward direction, I surmised this particular alignment was also a significant aspect of the meditation—that this specific positioning was most ideal for receiving answers for prayers directed to the Her.

Later in the dream, it was confirmed that each person attracts from the universe, realities that are aligned with their specific beliefs and values.

Eight days earlier, I'd dreamt (during the morning of 5-22-15), that I saw a steady stream of dark crimson-colored sand pouring down from some godlike, outstretched hand. It reminded me of the color of sand sometimes utilized to create Buddhist mandalas.

Beneath the hand, the granules of sand instantly began forming into the shape of a perfectly-formed chalice. Upon some thought, I wondered if this vision had been sent from Vajrayana Amitābha ("Amitābha" is translatable as "Infinite Light," hence Amitābha is also called "The Buddha of Immeasurable Life and Light").

Kuan Yin Buddhism

Kuan Yin had once proclaimed: *"As humans, you are learning to be as compassionate as I am. Call on me and I will help you to fully realize your compassionate nature. Just call on me and I will come! When someone works on their fear and anger, they can gain compassion. Fear always comes before anger. Still, many on earth will remain in their fear and anger until passing over. They have Free Will, so there is nothing that says they must heal their fear and anger. Yet, the ultimate answer is always compassion."~ Kuan Yin*

Then, in a dream on 3-5-15, I heard Kuan Yin confirm: *"It really is true! You are learning to be as compassionate as I am! Having true compassion is to understand another's pain and suffering from a place of strength and love. When you see/honor the light (the power) in others, you see/honor the light (the power) within yourself. In this way, you purify yourself, bringing the light of God into the world!"*

That summer, my husband, John, and I had placed a Kuan Yin statue on the alter in our living room. Beneath this beautiful

Kuan Yin Buddhism

porcelain statue of the deity, we periodically placed flowers and other offerings such as photos, names, or prayers for relatives and friends who may have been in need of Kuan Yin's help. During the autumn apple season, we'd each placed an apple before the statue. A few days later, I heard Kuan Yin say (between dreaming and waking): *"If you want me to truly appreciate the apple, you must cut it in half so I can enjoy its sweet aroma!"*. Amazed by that communication, I later cut both apples in half.

My dream of 5-19-15 revealed the deity, Kuan Yin, and myself standing on a mountain peak. I was enjoying the vista of a beautiful, golden sunset when suddenly in the dream, a garbage can appeared. *"You're focusing on the garbage can when you should be focusing on the sunset,"* scolded Kuan Yin. Earlier in that same dream I saw myself as very ill; about to have heart surgery. Realizing that even if the surgery was successful, I would be left with a fragile shell of my originally- healthy heart, I knew the

Kuan Yin Buddhism

dream was informing me that the human body does not thrive on sorrow and depression.

While in my waking life, I prided myself on having social awareness concerning the environment, human rights, etc., I knew the dream was asking me to "build my story" on only positive outcomes—that this is the way towards abundance and liberation!

Conversing with Kuan Yin in another dream, I then found myself flying through the universe; traveling here and there with Her. Incredibly, one of our stops was the hospital where my two children were born. Another was the Rocky Mountains.

In this pre-dawn vision, Kuan Yin's clear message to me was to show the power of love, compassion and gratitude; how these emotions not only assist one's waking reality but simultaneously elevate the vibration of one's entire spiritual family. Fully immersed in the knowledge that childbirth is a divine gift from the universe, I could actually feel how love and joy raise and amplify the vibration of one's entire spiritual family.

Appreciating each of my children's sacred souls, I broke down and wept with tears of joy and gratitude. Later, Kuan Yin and I were together just marveling at the beauty of the earth and in particular, the Rocky Mountains. There, my heart soared with feelings of wonderfully-expansive love and gratitude. Indeed, the intensity of my emotions caused my body to become totally animated; actually physically vibrating with waves of joy. My dream showed the divine interaction; how the human condition "creates divinity in the Higher Self".

Following that dream episode, I understood the concept of the "body electric". I knew that Kuan Yin was demonstrating that when we appreciate a moment, we sanctify it; elevating all energy levels of consciousness.

Years having passed after that amazing epiphany, I remembered a passage from <u>Oracle of Compassion: the Living Word of Kuan Yin</u>:

Kuan Yin Buddhism

"I'm going to wait for a moment because Kuan Yin is busy doing some things," mentioned Lena. *"She's doing some healing work on someone. I'm just going to sit with her, for a while, and watch what she is doing. She's working on someone who doesn't believe in healing. I warn her, saying, 'He doesn't believe in you!'"*

"It doesn't matter," Kuan Yin replied. *"Things work even if he doesn't believe in me."*

Then, on the morning of 8-19-19, upon waking, I experienced Kuan Yin's healing elixir as waves, like honey, seeping into my right temple and inward. Decades earlier, I'd been injured in this exact area and over the years, I'd experienced dizziness, headaches and my eyesight had been impaired. I'd always believed that miracles are nature unimpeded. Of course, Kuan Yin is known for pouring from Her bottle, Her magic healing elixir. Understanding how allowing Kuan Yin's elixir to penetrate injured areas of the body can bring comfort and healing, I heard Her say, *"Imagine my healing elixir penetrating any area of the body that needs healing. Believe and it will be so!"*

Kuan Yin Buddhism

Kuan Yin Buddhism

Section Three: The Kuan Yin Teachings

1. "You create the tree. You created your whole world with your thoughts. Say and believe that you can have the most divine life imaginable. Believe and be open to receiving. Focus upon your free will and your ability to create reality. I'm optimistic and hopeful you can do this." ~ Kuan Yin

2. "Look beyond what this world offers. Seek out another place beyond this earth. Be in the now. Where you are right now is what is important. Slow down. Everything is too chaotic. Lay down everything you need to do. You're not just your bodies, you know. Keep your spirit connection. Weight, chemicals of body are more influential when you're not connected with spirit. Connection with spirit can help overcome even genetic and hormonal limits." ~ Kuan Yin

Kuan Yin Buddhism

3. "Some believe I am in servitude to Buddha. However, Buddha doesn't see it that way. We're more like brother and sister. I'm showing, Lena, my abode, a place on earth where humans can visit me and be in my potency. Lena is looking at my statue and then at my form. There's a difference." ~ Kuan Yin

4. "I come to people in many forms, forms constructed from people's own perceptions of how I should come to them. And it is individual spiritual needs that create these unique perceptions. In the end, it does not matter what form I take." ~ Kuan Yin

5. "Unfortunately, many individuals really believe there are not enough resources for everyone. So many have made an 'agreement', then, that there isn't enough. War and any other dilemma focusing on hate, fear and murder is based on the belief in not enough and the illusion of survival of the fittest." ~ Kuan Yin

Kuan Yin Buddhism

6. "Many people are unaware they buy into this belief system. Nevertheless, they go on believing the only way they'll survive is to have money. The [above-discussed] oil families represent the majority's relationship with prosperity and survival. Humanity has created itself around the 'survival of the fittest' belief and the fearful belief that there are not enough resources." ~ Kuan Yin

7. "The greatest misunderstanding is to regard this life as a curse or punishment. Your experiences are ever changing, flowing, (so you won't take yourselves too seriously). It took a long time for your planet to evolve into this crisis. You are witnessing the greed and bad behavior of certain individuals. It is a very potent time. People are learning. And what they learn also sets them [the above-mentioned individuals] free. They will no longer be trapped in their own belief system. People will begin to get sparks of light. There will increasingly be more and more sparks which will erode the darkness of confusion." ~ Kuan Yin

Kuan Yin Buddhism

8. "It is not a matter of how much pain or suffering one might experience that deems one as worthy. It is not how productive one is, either. Everyone can access what they need from the *other side*. It's vital to living! Like blood in the body" ~ Kuan Yin

9. "This (earth) plane is stuck upon God looking a certain way and having certain teachings. God comes to us in many forms, many teachings." ~ Kuan Yin

10. " Unfortunately, wrong assumptions are made about suffering. Some individuals even believe that it is required, that suffering brings one closer to salvation. Quite the contrary," disputes Kuan Yin, "the God Force likes to play. Therefore, if all individuals could unite creating a real sense of community many problems could be healed. The reason pain exists is because of some of the choices you, as humans, have made. Humans always have a great freedom to choose." ~ Kuan Yin

Kuan Yin Buddhism

11. "Your senses as a human-being are relatively limited. Smells, tastes; there are dimensions you are not capable of knowing in the earth dimension." ~ Kuan Yin

12. "My specialty is healing." ~ Kuan Yin

13. "I can't save everyone. And I can only utilize humanity's own resources, which is love and Free Will. I can't use any force that does not come from within humans as a request to change the war. Just always value my words. The best motivation is valuing my words. We had to send the love and it is good. That is what prayer is. Many don't understand prayer. It is important to understand what prayer is. Prayer is sent out as strong intention and energy. Send focused intent. Be detached with the results. Trust! All of life is a prayer." ~ Kuan Yin

14. "There is a scene of Hiroshima, a great mushroom cloud. I'm inside it. Now it's

inside of me. Suddenly, it explodes in my body and I absorb it, *becoming* the energy. That is my message. Nothing can harm me! Even the most devastating force is changed, softened so that people will grow even when experiencing complete destruction. I'm not afraid to merge with the most fearsome creations. You see? I'm still in my original form. It didn't destroy me!" ~ Kuan Yin

15. "Being human is the most important thing in your existence. Your existence is eternal. This phase (of your soul) is so important because you learn so much in human form. This is where the individual's 'spark' of existence can expand into bigger, more powerful energies, not entities. Entities are closed systems whereas energies are open systems." ~ Kuan Yin

16. "Look at how they, the earth energies, suffer; how they die. Emerging from even the most tragic death, their energy keeps on going. Don't get sucked-in! Don't fall off that cliff; that suffering state of mind." ~ Kuan Yin

Kuan Yin Buddhism

17. "There really are demigods waiting in line to be born, to manifest as humans. In this way, they can evolve faster. You come to earth to further evolve." ~ Kuan Yin

18. "Some energies are not as potent. The only way to develop a potent energy is to spend an existence on the earth. There, one can develop a compassionate nature so that when passing onto other dimensions, one can be of help. When one leaves one's 'earth body' one will need to fully understand compassion to be helpful, effective. On earth, you are encapsulated in flesh. No soul is forced into an "assignment" upon the earth. Instead they go to their 'rightful space'. When you leave here you have a lot more power. It won't be ego-based power. Rather it will be beyond ego, beyond 'good and evil'. In fact, 'evil' is just a label as everything is intermixed. The pendulum just appears to swing back and forth." ~ Kuan Yin

19. "As far as suffering is concerned, those people have only experienced one part, the suffering part of their entire existence. It is not the end of their existence. They will continue to exist. The only reason for suffering is not being connected--being so far from the universe. Each of you has the potential for the God Force potency. However, no individual can overcome the God Force. There is a misinterpretation (by some) that Satan is as powerful as God. Limited energy cannot exist on its own. Every experience must exist and yet they (the limiting forces) can never exist on their own. Limited energy, then, is the experience of the absence of the God Force (as a teacher and as a belief). Therefore, there is no need to fear it. Those choosing such experiences have a need to understand how it feels to believe evil powers exist. Again, I say that those who pursue this route are taking it too personally. They believe the story they've made up about themselves." ~ Kuan Yin

20. "You want to taste all these experiences. And the ego makes it possible. Don't curse the ego. So many scriptures curse the ego self. Instead, regard your life as about choices, experiences and desire and that you are already liberated. Don't be afraid of desire. It is why you're here: to taste, live. It's just an 'agreement' you all made when you took on an ego. You splintered off from the whole." ~ Kuan Yin

21. "So many who make war are not yet in their full humanity. They hate their humanness as much as they appear to hate others. That is why certain religions can be harmful, at times." ~ Kuan Yin

22. "I want to emphasize here that only the body dies. People get too attached to their physicality. However, they have to. One's consciousness of the physical must be fairly strong in order for the soul's desire to continue. The more we feel our humanity, the more help we can give and the more joy we can create." ~ Kuan Yin

Kuan Yin Buddhism

23. "Many don't understand the power of love; that it is there for them if they choose to accept it. Of course, just because it's there, doesn't necessarily mean they'll accept it. Like a seed, it will always be there. Because of Free Will, humans can accept or reject that love. We, who so much wish to have the love we send be received, have to remain somewhat detached." ~ Kuan Yin

24. "Militarism can't happen without a dominant mindset, certain perceptions about the world, about other cultures. So many souls, energies have a certain perception of others. They believe they're separate from each other. Such perceptions can collect into an energy agreeing upon a specific direction the country will take. The lesson on earth is acceptance of differences. Don't forget you are a part of everything and everything is a part of you." ~ Kuan Yin

25. "As children mostly do not judge, nor do they intend harm, loving kindness is always easiest to express to them. Learning from this experience, one can begin to treat each person as if he were a child. After all, the only real thing one can do is to love and be loved. And as I've said before, mother's love is the closest to loving-kindness. Teach my message. *Practice my message.*" ~ Kuan Yin

26. "Don't forget to marvel at the wonders of the world. Gain strength. Suck up energy. Make a point to appreciate the fragrance of the flowers and the beauty of the sunset. It's like armor and then you're armed with an ability to be detached. One is meant to forgive, to forgive and be compassionate. Raise your voice in protest, while maintaining your detachment." ~ Kuan Yin

27. "One has to be very clear and perhaps even write things down. Work hard to make things clear and then review what you've learned. Nirvana, the path to Oneness, can be obtained

when identifying with Kuan Yin. We all have many deities, as we need their different qualities, *energies* to reach Oneness, the point of no identity." ~ Kuan Yin

28. "Human existence and human tendencies are wrapped in karma. It's not always going to be fair. Human nature isn't always fair. The main challenge is how to handle daily issues and still not hurt others. Always be reflective. Be honest and have integrity. One can utilize the divine tools (similar to the one's I am holding in my hands) and still maintain one's human nature." ~ Kuan Yin

29. "In this realm humans have to work very hard to be understood. They must be able to clearly communicate verbally and/or through writing. The human body and its communication tools are heavy and cumbersome compared to my realm." ~ Kuan Yin

30. "Human mistakes and inaccuracies are no less important than divinity. The human condition creates divinity in the higher self. Thus, it is very important to be human and not to shun or hate our humanity. The incredible process of being human allows for the higher self to *acknowledge and extract* divinity from one's trials and tribulations." ~ Kuan Yin

31. "Sometimes it's okay to go inside and work on your own personal issues rather than being so concerned about the outside realm. You know that I can't interfere with karma. The karmic cycle is just. However, one can ride karma like a wave. I have the tools and everyone can choose to utilize them to improve their lives. Sometimes the waves are small. Sometimes the waves are big. In order to help others, one must learn how to help oneself." ~ Kuan Yin

32. "Hatred is not helpful at all. In fact, it's unnatural. And it is really not the truth. The truth is one must be fully human for the divine

part of self to be more in tune. Rejecting the human body assures one will have to come back, return to the lessons here on earth. It means 'you didn't get it'!" ~ Kuan Yin

33. "Most contemporary religions 'don't get it'. The indigenous tribes are the most powerful as many of them are so in harmony with nature as to be really, really divinely human. They're so in touch with their humanity that they're totally in tune with their diva nature. They know that human/nature harmony is the crux of spirituality." ~ Kuan Yin

34. "Humans say they're better than each other. And they say they're better than *nature*. It's ludicrous to compare the intelligence of other living creatures to human intelligence. Plants have enormous intelligences and spirituality. However, the 'better than' mindset greatly contributes to the ongoing environmental destruction." ~ Kuan Yin

35. "The earth is trying to teach humans that everything is spirit. Eventually, humans will learn. It's just another way to understand divinity. Spirit works through one's own humanity and the earth. Everything here on earth is for the divine evolution of *all* energies. Whereas the word 'beings' so often refers only to humans, I use the term 'energies' as it encompasses all living things on the planet." ~ Kuan Yin

36. "You can't change people. You can love them and give to them. If they can't receive it's not a reason not to love them, unless impossible conditions have been set upon the relationship, unless it is a kind of conditional love. Look at Christ. The saints! Jesus came with a message. Humanity is still feeling sorry for him. He's not feeling sorry for himself." ~ Kuan Yin

37. "It's important to accept that the human condition is temporary, fleeting. It's filled with pain and suffering, beauty, strange tastes,

Kuan Yin Buddhism

odors of death; *everything* that exists in the universe." ~ Kuan Yin

38. "Sometimes parents don't want their children to watch certain cartoons. However, there's an important message one can glean from these episodes. For example, Wile E. Coyote can get blown up. After that, he may get squished by a bunch of rocks. Over and over he can defy destruction. How many times are you going to feel sorry for him when he keeps coming back?" ~ Kuan Yin

39. "Death is like giving birth. Birth can be painful. Sometimes women die from giving birth. However, when the baby is born, all that pain (that was endured) vanishes in an instant. Love for that tiny baby makes one forget the pain, the fear. And as I've said before, love between mother and child is the highest experience, the closest to divine love. You might wonder about the parallel I'm making between birth and death. But I say to you, the fear and pain accompanying an awful death is over

quickly. Beyond that portal one is suddenly in the light, in oneness and bliss. Some women are powerful teachers. However, even women can be afraid of death, forget how the pain vanishes. Just as a woman heals rapidly after childbirth and then is able to fall in love with her baby, those who pass over also are able to fall in love with a new life." ~ Kuan Yin

40. "No two paths look the same. Tradition is good. However, in Western Cultures there are so many people looking for wisdom. And it is important to get familiar with the various paths. Such a process develops character for one to look inward for their right path." ~ Kuan Yin

41. "People who've never suffered haven't yet developed an ability to utilize their own creativity to solve a challenging situation. An analogy would be that of a person who has fallen into a well. After many attempts of trying to climb out of the well, they develop strength, ingenuity. That is what many are doing on this

earth. However, devastating struggle is always karmic. It might seem karmic if one has had a bad day or week. However, 'little suffering' is for the purpose of building character and inner trust. On the other hand, 'extreme suffering' for no apparent reason is an indication one is dealing with *big karma*." One usually finds a deity or god, which can help liberate, teach them. It is not helpful, however, to have a deity *forced* upon one. It may be the *wrong angel*—the *wrong guide*. In such a case, the guide or religion can have the effect of having the individual not perceive *anything* spiritual or cause them to believe they've failed. Unfortunately, sometimes in these instances, individuals will shun their own spiritual path." ~ Kuan Yin

42. "There really are demigods waiting in line to be born, to manifest as humans. In this way, they can evolve faster. It is so, then, that everyone comes to earth to further evolve." ~ Kuan Yin

43. "I see the folds of her garment, again, so thick and intricate. Kuan Yin is here observing a lotus. However, she's more than observing it; she's being with it, meditating upon it, appreciating it. She's focused very intently on the lotus as if she is conversing with it. It's an interesting thing to see Kuan Yin relating to a flower so intently. Now, the lotus is floating away." ~ Lena Lees

44. "There is a Buddhist parable. It involves an individual who climbs the mountain to receive wisdom from a monk. If one comes to the monk with an empty container, that individual can be filled with wisdom. On the other hand, if one comes *filled* with preconceptions, their mind already made up; any new knowledge or wisdom will simply spill over. The best state of meditation is to come to these sessions with an 'empty cup'. Then you can receive new information without any forced structure or chronology. Hope learned not to 'jam her cup' with too much intellectualism. It closes off the heart. Think of the head as the top of the bottle.

Kuan Yin Buddhism

If it is too tightly, firmly 'screwed on', it closes off the entire *vessel*. The message, then, is to not *lose your head*. If the head is 'lost', true wisdom, knowledge cannot reach the heart." ~ Kuan Yin

45. "You don't have to follow Buddhist scriptures. Just see my image, *create* my image. Understand all my manifestations. Watch my pastimes." ~ Kuan Yin

46. "Even the earth is reflective of the different kinds of evolution. There is the hellish aspect, deserts and other unlivable places. There are places on the earth where people get hurt. However, there are also places of incredible peace and beauty. All of these Evolutionary Potentials are being played out at the same time, somewhere on the earth. You can come to that place of peace." ~ Kuan Yin

47. "All anyone has the power to do is to develop their faith and trust. It is all anyone can do to understand the Grand Plan. There is life and

there is karma. There are so many levels of existence. Different people live on different levels. Everything is very individualized. Those who do not believe may deny all of this because it's too complicated." ~ Kuan Yin

48. "This is the very reason the saints don't immediately enter Nirvana. Even after they've attained perfect enlightenment, they cannot abide the thought of even one soul suffering. That is why you, Lena, are still here on the earth." ~ Kuan Yin

49. "Humanity has *created itself around* the "survival of the fittest" belief and the fearful belief *that there is not enough.* Unfortunately, many individuals really believe there are not enough resources for everyone." ~ Kuan Yin

50. "At the same time you're equal to everyone else, you need to know you're also special, unique. Everyone has his or her own uniqueness while also being equal to the next person." ~ Kuan Yin

Kuan Yin Buddhism

51. "It's a good time to ask ourselves to look at the lies we are telling ourselves. It's a time to examine our thoughts and the thoughts of the people of the world. Let us all reflect upon the great mix of free will and karma. Reread the past chapters and ponder what I have said. Karma is intricate, detailed. One cannot dwell on only one particle of this great collective energy. Your life is but one frame of an entire reel of film. Everyone has their part. Some don't perform any of their part as they have incomplete or incorrect belief systems. Sometimes it seems as if this world is completely chaotic and sometimes it really is. However, there is a corrective force, an actual physical force." ~ Kuan Yin

52. "Develop your faith and trust. Do not drag the negative past or future into the present. Understanding the possibilities of the present. It's a skill useful for discovering the divine." ~ Kuan Yin

53. "There is a tube—a diagram. One end is the past, the other the future. The middle of the tube, the present, is your way, your *vehicle* for changing reality. You slip into the universe, while living in this dream, this present. Your escape hatch is *right here.* It's like meditating upon a beautiful place. The more one dwells on the vision of the beautiful place, the more real it becomes." ~ Kuan Yin

54. "Thoughts influence the way the world can go. What a radical concept! Everyone having loving kindness! With practice, a reality is created somewhere having that very consciousness of loving kindness. Such practice also draws one to those (loving kindness) planes of consciousness. If you were just to look to the children as examples for living you're lives, you would know what to do. Everything we learn from them, we can apply to the world. It would be wonderful if all of society could do this: approach and resolve issues in such an innocent way." ~ Kuan Yin

55. "The male energy is out of control, too concentrated in the world. It's as if there's too much spice or too much sugar in the recipe. It is to a point where no one can eat or digest it anymore. This concentration of male energy is beyond extreme bitterness or some other unpleasant taste. It is like butter that has become rancid, stagnation of the original essence of yang energy. Running cultures through this (stagnant male) energy no longer generates positive effects." ~ Kuan Yin

56. "You might believe that the act of relating to a flower appears to be so simple. Yet, it takes a tremendous amount of courage to make such a 'simple' act important." ~ Kuan Yin

57. "Love will keep finding that issue, the one that has you running. Sometimes it isn't those issues that make one want to leave the relationship. Instead, maybe one or both partners have completed the assignment. Whatever is not finished, however, will be repeated again and again in future

relationships. It is the law of karma. Karma does not make any distinction between this life and the next. It repeats and repeats until the soul evolves. It removes the dust, the layers, making free that which was imprisoned. The best you can do is to live a life governed by integrity. Live your life with authenticity. Do the best you can and be honest with yourself and others. There is a collective agreement that this (life you are living on earth) is the only reality. Therefore, you have to play along." ~ Kuan Yin

58. "Do not believe that your humanity prevents you from being spiritual. Know that this (earth) drama doesn't mean spirituality doesn't exist on the earth plane. Try to be forgiving and objective when enduring your own earthly drama. Indeed, one's approach to one's own life drama can actually affect the outcome. That is, certain interactive strategies can render an ordinary drama, spiritual. Don't fall into the trap of ego and money. Don't be too concerned whether the drama you're experiencing is a result of karma. Rather, emphasize the concept

Kuan Yin Buddhism

that we are all One and that no one is better than the other. You are all sacred energies and everyone is as sacred as the next." ~ Kuan Yin

59. "When one brings spirit into the human realm, it can even *spiritualize* matter. Matter can then become lighter, indeed *liberated*; not as dense as before. Those souls who've chosen that path (as monks) are trying to bring spirit into matter. Instead of pushing paper all day, they perform the rituals and ceremonies. However, the peasant woman who stays home all day is no less important or less spiritual than the monks. Anyone can bring spirit into her daily life. Being a monk is just one choice." ~ Kuan Yin

60. "I felt Kuan Yin in my heart. She was immense, having thousands of arms. In each hand was a symbol, tools for understanding our lives. She was grasping different things like a candle, the Buddha, hands with eyes, a lotus, the Buddhist symbol for peace, her bottle containing healing elixir; instruments which are

for peacefully slaying injustice, the fog of indecision. These are instruments for one's protection, as well." ~ Lena Lees

61. "There is the clean and clear wealth of higher consciousness. It is devoid of the depraved energy that can be attached to money. This is the pure wealth—the wealth of higher consciousness. There is a dimension (plane of consciousness) where that pure wealth of consciousness is a reality. It is reality where everyone is loved, where everyone is fed and healthy." ~ Kuan Yin

62. "I delight in helping to liberate souls. I don't like suffering. However suffering reminds me of the work I need to do to help people. Liberating individuals from their suffering is my primary motivation. Of course, the reasons for suffering are as personal and varied as one's voice or thoughts. Humankind needs to understand that suffering is just (and people *accept* it because of higher reasons) and that no one is a victim. ~ Kuan Yin"

63. "Just let the mind go and look at a flower. Parents are god-like in their power over children. Your parent's lives were also lived in fear. However, there are realms where there is absolutely no fear. In such divine realms, realization is complete. Fear is completely absent from these realms. On this earth where people can feel so separate, there does not exist a feeling of Oneness. I know ultimately nothing can harm or destroy you. Fear comes from not knowing the entire truth." ~ Kuan Yin

64. "The reasons for suffering are as personal and varied as one's voice or thoughts. Humankind needs to understand that suffering is just (and indeed, people *accept* it because of higher reasons). No one is a victim. There are layers and layers—coat upon coat of denseness. This is the human condition. It is similar to the hundred thousand lenses comprising a bee's eye. Some scientists (such as Einstein) are very spiritual. They have already begun to explore

and understand this approach to reality." ~ Kuan Yin

65. "There is a woman who is crying. She has layers and layers of, not mist, but similar to different shades of thick and gooey gray lacquer that have been clinging to this woman for hundreds of years. Underneath all of these layers is the woman's pure soul essence, that part of her which knows the processes it will take for her to be released from her karma, that part of her which knows *everything*. This is the element of self that agrees to suffering and knows the woman cannot be destroyed. And though this woman's reality may appear unjust some 'unjust bomb' cannot blow her up. It cannot destroy her essence, her *Core Being*." ~ Kuan Yin

66. "The trauma of everyday living can cause the chakras to get shoved around, disconnected. When resting, one can benefit from light touches to the heart, stomach and head, connecting the chakras to one another and also

from the inside out. Life is so intense. It can scatter one's energy. Please don't be afraid of making mistakes. In fact, no step can be a 'misstep'." ~ Kuan Yin

67. "When individuals and society don't perceive the mother as important, there will always be as a result, a disproportionate amount of obesity and stomach problems. Here, I want to stress that the stomach, not the heart, is the center of our beings. Some might believe because love and emotions spring from the heart, that it is the heart that directs (and is at the center of) our lives. However, it is important to remember that it is the stomach which defines our energy field and our identity—everything. Think of those societies, tribes, where a large stomach denotes wealth and power. It is no accident. You identify yourselves through your stomachs. However, because of how your culture holds motherhood in low esteem, your culture is out of balance. Life is so intense. It can scatter one's energy. When there is so much pain in the heart, it naturally

migrates to the stomach. The pain goes to the stomach because the navel (and all that it represents, maternal comfort and nurturing) is there. In fact, this pain is stored in the stomach until the issues causing the pain are finally resolved." ~ Kuan Yin

68. "Certain body types correlate with certain emotional issues. Those who are overweight often crave nurturing, motherly love. While we all need nurturing, those who are obese may have a greater karmic need and (in some cases) may have lost their mother in a past life. Overeating and binging and purging can be attempts by the individual to replace the nurturance of the umbilical cord. For some, it may be that they were not nursed long enough. For others, they could have been separated from their mothers too soon. The mother was not necessarily wrong. Instead, the circumstances surrounding the child's upbringing did not meet the nurturing needs of that particular individual…In the world, the mothering element is not valued enough.

Perhaps, if motherly love were more valued there would be less obesity." ~ Kuan Yin

69. "You have, at least, five brainwave frequency ranges for your survival. They are the built-in defenses of human consciousness. Similar to the layers, *auras* around the body they represent layers of consciousness. The various brainwaves help you go beyond, *under* the layers of karma." ~ Kuan Yin

70. "It's not a catastrophe that the earth is dying. Actually, things are right on schedule. Your precious earth cannot be destroyed, it just *looks* that way. There is planetary karmic build-up. It's nothing the planet did: more like a pattern of energy on the planet. Whenever an event occurs, there is a 'planetary imprint'. Energies are drawn to that imprint. Similar energies are then drawn to the existing energies." ~ Kuan Yin

71. "The energies that are here on earth have Free Will. When you mix Free Will you get

certain deviants. It is intended to be a planet for this purpose. Earth represents a certain grade similar to a school. It's all a grand experiment. It's possible to completely re-create this earth. You'll kill yourselves before you kill the earth. We're talking in dualities because dualities are built into your language. You think that just because there is an absence of good, for instance, that evil exists. This is not so. In fact, things are far more intricate." ~ Kuan Yin

72. "These protective elements (the brainwaves) help your human bodies function and survive on this earth plane. However, this discussion involves the soul. Gravity holds your physical bodies in place. Your skin holds the spirit in place. Heavy layers of energy, karma (around the earth and the body), weigh you down. Every layer is different. The brain waves represent the different layers of consciousness. Each brainwave is a sort of gelatinous substance; layer upon layer; much like the onionskin metaphor. Accessing a certain layer accesses

certain abilities [i.e. trance skills in the alpha range, dream abilities in the theta range, etc.]. They all work together perfectly. When an individual "hits" a certain layer, he can work (heal) certain issues. The sense of time in one world is not the same as in another world." ~ Kuan Yin

73. "The pain in those chakras is meant to be felt; experienced. You are going to feel it (the sadness, and despair) move. It's part of the 'push-through'. The energy in the solar plexus, especially, needs to move." ~ Kuan Yin

74. "Here is a picture of someone running with sandbags. When the person finally lets-go of the sandbags, he or she is faster, stronger. That's what the earth existence is like. In many ways living on earth is an 'artificial burden'. Once one is free of their body, they're not only lighter; they are also stronger, more powerful." ~ Kuan Yin

Kuan Yin Buddhism

75. "Balance. Practice. Meditating upon my form. These are three excellent spiritual practices to put my teachings in place. Spirituality is a focus, a commitment, not a punishment. It's liberating." ~ Kuan Yin

76. "Love will keep finding that issue, the one that has you running. One can bring spirit into the 'space' of the human body…Being human is an opportunity to bring spirit into all that is material. Be willing to go to the lightness. Don't feed off what is not right in the world." ~ Kuan Yin

77. "Prosperity can happen at any time. I want to give you everything that you need. Focus on that symbol (the diamond) of prosperity. Taking that first step is what you need. Say and believe that more and more you can have all the possibilities. It is your mantra. I want you to believe and be open to receiving. Perhaps you can imagine a crystal in the place of a real diamond. Focus upon it and breathe in what it represents (its energy) to those areas of the

body that need healing. Practice the meditation of seeing me holding and giving you this huge, chunky diamond. Remember, this diamond doesn't just represent material wealth. Its myriad facets also represent consciousness, love and all other forms of abundance. Practice receiving it." ~ Kuan Yin

78. "For any person, a certain bodily organ can be the source of nightmares. Each person, of course is unique. A person might mention they've experienced a nightmare. The nightmare may be trying to inform the person a certain organ needs particular nutrients, elements. As we've discussed, the chakras also need particular nutrients, elements. Certain emotions also *live* in the chakras. Limiting emotions can block off certain areas of the body. An individual, then, can utilize this approach (hypnosis and dream analysis) as a possible preventive medicine warding off illness in certain prone areas of the body." ~ Kuan Yin

Kuan Yin Buddhism

79. "I wish someone would do sound tuning of the chakras. Sound comes first in the universe. You're all made of sound. (*Kuan Yin then described a computerized devise that could measure and adjust the sound vibration for each chakra.*) It would be like having one's hearing checked. Only one would be working with the energy centers—the chakras. Individuals could get more in touch with their own pulses and their relationship with sound. It would feel really good and could possibly be used for pain management. There will be in the coming years a proportionally larger group of the elderly in your society. People will live longer. However, they will have many misalignments in the chakras. Sound therapy could be very soothing as well as help an individual to adjust, to be ready to move on to their next life." ~ Kuan Yin

80. "I come to each person in a different form. Sometimes, I will come even in the crudest of forms if it leads people to their rightful path. I provide whatever one's soul wants, whatever one is ready for or evolved to. It's very difficult

to keep certain beings on this planet. For those who've come from higher planes and had access to other, more heightened senses, experiences here can make the earth feel like a prison." ~ Kuan Yin

81. Here in the bamboo garden. Kuan Yin is very illuminated. Her garment is so bright, so filled with light. She's holding a musical instrument. I think it is a lute. Completely focused upon tuning this instrument—trying to get the sound just right, She does not speak. Eventually She says, "Once this instrument is correctly tuned and kept tuned any amount of chaos won't matter, won't influence it. This, of course, is Kuan Yin's metaphor for keeping the body chakras well-tuned. This teaching is a continuation of Her message concerning the effects of sound and vibrations upon physicality. She is also saying that the power of sound (and pulse) is why music is so calming and comforting."

Kuan Yin Buddhism

82. "I want you to take the diamond, receive all that it stands for. Maybe you can hold a large crystal and imagine it as the diamond. When you place this imaginary diamond on your solar plexus, visualize its potency and value, the highest and safest feelings going into your stomach. I want you to bring light into your body. Practice that." ~ Kuan Yin

83. Above the thick and heavy atmosphere are astonishingly vivid colors of bright light. "Push it aside. It is like the Biblical "parting of the waters"!" commands Kuan Yin. "Only this is parting of dense consciousness. It's the only way to keep you in balance during the difficult times. The only way to remain strong is to pray for others. Don't get too depleted."

84. "There is endless light; endless possibilities. It is an infinite light that goes on forever. It's astounding. It is so much more powerful than any darkness humans create." ~ Kuan Yin

Kuan Yin Buddhism

85. "One reason you might not take to heart and practice these techniques ardently is that you don't believe that you're valuable. Another is that you don't have enough faith. It's all about faith." ~ Kuan Yin

86. "The only way to fully utilize your human experience is to practice some kind of meditation or visualization. It does work. People really need it. It's the only way to get through the difficult times. This kind of practice puts us in the 'Kuan Yin Spirit'. You're the *Watcher*. Instead of judging, you just see. Whether meditating upon my form or bringing light into the chakras, all these techniques will help you in your life." ~ Kuan Yin

87. "A really powerful thing to do a meditation that involves surrounding a person with light. It's also powerful to explore hypnosis and chakra alignment techniques. Letting go of former beliefs and impressions and seeing what can be learned about yourself and others helps with compassion. The individual meditated

upon will feel the good intentions—that you want the highest good for them. Of course it's also beneficial for the one who is meditating." ~ Kuan Yin

88. "Just be with the fact that life is always changing but that humans always have the ability to live in the moment. It is not so important about the end, resolution of the problem, rather it is how you are *with it*; how you *interact* with it…This 'birthing' is a learning process. This learning process (problem) involves constant giving, learning, receiving, responding, taking in and interpreting processes. Let's see what happens next. Not even God knows. Let me restate that! The cool thing about free will is that even if one has a huge bag of karma there is still a lot of free will for all those souls coming into the world. Stop looking at the half-empty glass. Remember to make lemonade from lemons as the saying instructs us to do. Just practice being in the moment." ~ Kuan Yin

Kuan Yin Buddhism

89. "It's a perfect Buddhist time. Your hopes have been dashed. Your cup has been overturned. Some of the aspects of your life have not gone the way you had hoped. However, some of the stagnant energy has been cleared away. It is time to regroup. Everything is on schedule. The outcome is not important. What is important is that those who gave their energy and time *seized* the moment. Don't have an attachment to the outcome. Do the right thing because it is the right thing to do such as helping others, helping the earth." ~ Kuan Yin

90. "It is not up to you to fix others. It is up to the spirit guides. You have to turn it over to them. Stop trying to be a 'super-being'. Turn over your tendency to fix him, help him. These thoughts and impressions have been with this person for such a long time that he has created a *deeply-ingrained karmic loop*. Now it's so deep, it is difficult for him to *climb out* of it. A humble mantra: 'I can't fix others'." ~ Kuan Yin

Kuan Yin Buddhism

91. "I'm suddenly feeling really weak, heavy," confides Lena, from an ever-deepening trance. "Kuan Yin is taking me to a place representing a certain kind of collective consciousness. It is an actual reality but is also symbolic of powerless women living on the earth. I seem to be in Afghanistan (or somewhere resembling Afghanistan) but am also aware this area represents the repressive reality in many parts of the world. I'm experiencing the intense feelings of defeat in the women. However, I'm also feeling the extreme fear of women by the men. Why are the men so terrified of women? Somehow, they feel vulnerable. Kuan Yin is showing me some kind of divide. One side holds the terrified men. The other side holds the defeated, powerless women. This, for now, is as much as I'm able to interpret." ~ Lena Lees

92. "Spiders are patient and meticulous. Human sometimes believe insects are insignificant because they are small. However, their work is of great importance to the world. Be still and watch the spider build its web." ~ Kuan Yin

93. "Don't be too hard on yourself about your choices in life. When one subtracts (from the equation of life) physical birth and death, one can regard lessons learned as forming an infinite line. Then one can say, 'I'm learning this right now'. Try to crystallize the components of the lesson, excluding as much as is possible gender and financial factors. Repeat to yourself, 'this is the lesson I'm learning right now, at this exact moment in time'." ~ Kuan Yin

94. "What makes any kind of relationship begin and then work is an initial communication. Following the initial communication there is always an adjustment. For example, someone has a question. Whatever information is exchanged impacts both the person who has presented the question and the person who responds. Information has been shared and everyone involved makes some kind of an adjustment. There are constant adjustments resulting from communication." ~ Kuan Yin

95. "When one feels pulled to do a particular thing, when one has passion for a certain life path, karma is always involved. In such an instance, when the goal is worthy and makes one happy, one should continue on that same life path. Continue down the path that makes you feel fulfilled. Those who continue on an unrewarding path for the sake of only monetary gain are displaying a lack of trust in life. Continuing in such a mistrustful way will only bring impoverishment. Following one's heart, continuing on one's divine path, ultimately brings abundance." ~ Kuan Yin

96. "Living in places like the one you are experiencing right now [some location in China], exuding a natural and intense spirituality brings one closer to a simpler kind of life. While remnants of Western Culture can still seep in, these places remain largely unchanged from their ancient traditions. I'd like you to experience this place (physically go here)

Kuan Yin Buddhism

as it will make you more whole, able to help others." ~ Kuan Yin

97. "Those who do not believe, who proclaim themselves as atheists, may want to deny all of this because it's too complicated...I feel sadness for your culture. Overly engrossed, invested in the birth-death cycle, many don't understand that this is chosen at a Soul (Core) Essence level. Learn from the Elders, those Speakers who came before me. Come to know the basic universal principles. Be open to new learning opportunities. Loving people is the most helpful thing anyone can do." ~ Kuan Yin

98. "Kuan Yin is showing me visually how I'm (we all are) part of a round ball of light that people call God," delineates Lena. "There are those who would rather God were thought of as a person, a man with a white beard," elaborates Kuan Yin. "However, for purposes of this manuscript, I will continue with this ball of light analogy of the God Force." "I'm seeing not pie-shaped but straight slivers coming from this

Kuan Yin Buddhism

central ball of light," depicts Lena. "These straight slivers of light become a person who plays out adventures from their beliefs. When you put all the slivers together they form God. It is as if one takes a small chip of gold from a cave made of gold. The cave and chip of gold are separate. Yet, they are the same. How can this be?"

Answering her own question, Lena comments, "Because they are both comprised of the same chemical elements. Why do we even go through such a complex process? Is it all just a beautiful game?" Lena asks Kuan Yin. "The God Force likes intense pleasure," expounds Kuan Yin. "However, the God Force experiences itself more clearly when it can separate itself out; obtaining a different point of view. Because of this separation, [becoming human--the personification of the "Always Self"], there is the possibility for pain."

99. "Experiential versus the God eye! Possessing 'ego vision', a person's view through their physical eyes can be quite versatile, able to

Kuan Yin Buddhism

discern wide and varied vistas over huge distances; scrutinizing the minutest of details. Ego's very nature: capable of relatively expansive, detailed, and yet individualistic perspective is crucial. Separating itself out from the God Force, ego extracts infinite unique experiences, integral to humanity's process of spiritualizing matter. Incarnating on the earth, achieving individualism is therefore crucial for attaining divinity. Individualism, though, may cause momentary estrangement from the God Self. Intent on seeking their individualism, a person could forget that they are everything in the mirror; the 'sliver' and the 'ball of light'." ~ Kuan Yin

100. "Humans are absorbed in 'tasting' everything that shows up during the journey. However, one cannot taste everything without eventually getting a bellyache! Compared to the other spiritual realms, human senses are quite limited. In these other realms there are more senses, more enjoyment. However, even in these other realms the ego wants to hold onto

things, situations. Our spirit knows we don't die nor are we born. If our ego knew what our greater self knows, it would not fear disaster. Caught up in a new incarnation, one may forget their Always State/Form; perhaps forgetting everything from before. However, you are already, always that! There is only eternity, knowledge and bliss. But one could still be terrified that it might not be true. That is ego at work. Ego can keep one from being free." ~ Kuan Yin

101. "You want to taste all these experiences. And the ego makes it possible. Don't curse the ego. So many scriptures curse the ego self. Instead, look at your life as about choices, experiences and desires--that you are already liberated. Don't be afraid of desire. That is why you're here, to taste, *live*. The God force likes to play. Therefore, if all individuals could unite, creating real community, all problems could be healed." ~ Kuan Yin

102. "The God force is separate and not separate, whole and not whole at the same time. Really, it is not 'sliceable', not reducible. Even when it is sliced into individual energies, it does not diminish the total God force *or* the power of the individual. Each of you has the potential for the God force potency. However, no individual can *overcome* the God force. There is a misinterpretation, that Satan is as powerful as God. Limited energy cannot live on its own." ~ Kuan Yin

103. "Please avoid taking even life's positive accomplishments or identities too personally, as well. People can get stuck in similar lifetimes, identifying too strongly with even an incarnation's positive achievements and personas. Clinging to any past identity [expansive or limiting], then, acts as a roadblock, preventing one from progressing to other 'flavors' [beliefs and their experiences]." ~ Kuan Yin

Kuan Yin Buddhism

104. "When Kuan Yin refers to 'reality', she really means truth, the importance of life," explains Lena Lees. Kuan Yin responds: "Some need to practice distancing themselves from materialism while others need to get more grounded in the material world." ~ Lena Lees

105. "I want to emphasize that you are in the 'printed word' of your humanity. There is an *energetic reaction* to something in print. That is what is meant by *the power of the word*. There is even a reaction from the universe to the energetic quality of the book. Writers know this. From such reactions, another and another energy is created. The 'power of the word', then, cannot be triggered until the book is actually in print." ~ Kuan Yin

106. "Unless one fully experiences one's 'full humanity', one will have to experience earth again and again. One will have to repeat the lessons offered here upon the earth. It is possible that one need not have to reincarnate. However, many don't live up to their full

potential because they're afraid of death." ~ Kuan Yin

107. "The reality I'm showing you represents pure wealth. No greed is involved. Beings in this dimension desire this pure wealth because it feels good; it expands their consciousness. This is a very different approach from desiring to keep all the resources for oneself; to say that others can't have it and to also believe there is not enough." ~ Kuan Yin

108. "One can't just 'hit life' and expect it will co-operate, go exactly the way one wants. Maybe it will and maybe it won't. You might have heard the sayings, 'the path is the goal' or 'the journey is the goal'. These sayings are antithetical to the reality of living in your culture. Your culture is very goal structured. There is always a push to be where one is supposed to be rather than savoring where one is right now. This is cultural, not instinctual. Naturally, one needs a driving force to survive. However, the concept of having specific goals is very Western.

Kuan Yin Buddhism

This kind of mindset makes people very ambitious. However, no one is obligated to live her/his life by this point of view. It's important to have an idea of the path one wants to be on. This statement comes with the warning that one not be too attached to the outcome." ~ Kuan Yin

109. "To have a concept about the nature of one's life path can be a skillful tool in living one's life. However there is a danger that one will misconstrue a goal to be the entire purpose of one's life and in so doing perhaps create a negative driving force." ~ Kuan Yin

110. "Kuan Yin believes that praying for other's well-being is the most incredible thing a person can do. There is something else. Because Kuan Yin is made of pure intention, she is energized by the good intention and prayers of people." ~ Lena Lees

111. "Those magical powers you had as a child (and still have) originated from your Authentic

Kuan Yin Buddhism

Self. This Authentic Self is the part of you that lives before and after this lifetime--that is eternal." ~ Kuan Yin

112. "The *agreement*, then, is to go on believing in that particular flavor. Here's where reincarnation and its opportunity for experiencing a vast array of perspectives, "agreements", enters in. Another life offers another opportunity, a chance to *switch flavors*, so to speak. Taking oneself too personally, however, can cause a soul to get caught up, stuck in redundancy: in a particular (and unfortunate) flavor. In such instances, the individual is forgetting he has the ability to *choose* his flavors, her/his lives." ~ Kuan Yin

113. "Appreciate and marvel at everything! Especially nature! Learn from nature. Learn the way it works so you can know how to be in the world. Remember to marvel at the wonders of the world when you've had enough, for the time being, of the human realm. Science helps one marvel. Scientists might not think of

themselves as being spiritual. However, the knowledge they bring to the world is very spiritual. There are marvels under the sea. There are great examples in nature of how to behave, live in harmony. Observe, for example, the geese, how they fly fixed in perfect chevron formation, while winging their way towards their destination." ~ Kuan Yin

114. "Every experience must exist…[Incorporating a narrow-minded approach] is similar to a person going into an ice cream store and only choosing one flavor from many. Preoccupied with tasting that flavor for a very long time, they are probably quite sick and tired of it. Still, they don't want to believe there are any other flavors available." ~ Kuan Yin

115. "Kuan Yin tells me we are all spiritual beings who have taken birth here. She says the earth plane is a wonderful opportunity to develop humility and compassion." ~ Lena Lees

Kuan Yin Buddhism

116. "Some of the media available in your culture tend to go after one's emotions. Fear, sadness and anxiety can make money for these interests. When people watch, allowing themselves to be manipulated by such limiting visions and emotions, they feed the 'machine'. Instead, immerse yourself in the beauty of the world. Begin with marveling at the beauty of nature. Art and music nurture and balance the self. Indulge yourself with every art that engages the senses. Take shelter in the arts. Taste, touch and smell: anything that uses and appeals to the senses! There are, as other examples of creative outlets, the culinary arts and working with flowers."~ Kuan Yin

117. "Maybe you can hold a large crystal and imagine it as the diamond. When you place this imaginary diamond on your solar plexus, visualize its potency and value—the highest and safest feelings going into your stomach…I want you to bring that light into your body. Practice that." ~ Kuan Yin

118. "Say and believe...Imagine the possibilities of something greater than is right here...Don't be too concerned whether the drama you're experiencing is a result of karma. Rather, emphasize the concept that we are all one, that no one is better than the other. You are all sacred energies and everyone is as sacred as the next." ~ Kuan Yin

119. "Let the magic happen! It is always there. Abundance and love are always there. Believe in the highest good. There is a higher essence to everything. The realm you're in has a heaviness that mutes energy. You can penetrate through it, no matter how dark and heavy. Sometimes it has nothing to do with karma. Just don't forget to keep it open. Don't get too bogged down...Prosperity can happen at any time. I want to give you everything that you need." ~ Kuan Yin

120. "I'm seeing a beautiful beam of light. It represents the oneness of human consciousness." ~ Lena Lees

Kuan Yin Buddhism

121. "You've already lived any future lives, all of your lives! There is no such thing as time! Humans need not take everything that happens to them and around them so personally. Such an approach to living can create pain." ~ Kuan Yin

122. "Some people believe that death is a punishment from God rather than a natural progression, a doorway to other realities. By having such a grim perspective, they make it a fearful and painful experience. I repeat! Just don't take everything so personally. In fact, if humans didn't cling to events in their lives, every experience that ever was could be lived in an instant. However, it is often the nature of ego to grab at everything. It doesn't want to let go. The ego's fear of letting go can be compared to a fear of falling." ~ Kuan Yin

123. "Instead of seeing things and events separately, we should perceive them as part of the whole. Conversely, Kuan Yin is saying we

also forget to notice the little things, a single stone or grain of sand. So, the existential question is: when to notice the little things and when to see things as a whole. A powerful meditation is when contemplating the oneness of everything is to find something's unique qualities. For example, observing an island's wholeness and then focusing upon the uniqueness of a single stone. Westerners are dealing with this dichotomy on a grand scale. However, Kuan Yin wants me to emphasize that this meditation is simple but powerful. It's like physical exercise. One can practice it just once a day or as often as one likes. Other examples to meditate upon (other than an individual stone on the island beach) are faces in a crowd or a leaf on a tree. Each person (in the crowd) is unique and yet (at that very moment) part of the whole. The same is true for leaves on the trees. Practicing this deceptively easy meditation helps each of us to see reality." ~ Lena Lees

Kuan Yin Buddhism

124. "Try to be here, right now. Focus upon a leaf fluttering, light reflected on the waves. Things are more beautiful, afterwards. Make it your own experience. Things will taste, feel better. Colors will be brighter and you'll feel more alive. It is the only thing that is real." ~ Kuan Yin

125. "Festivals are joyous. They are a way to celebrate the beauty of the local culture and the camaraderie between the citizens. Participate in local festivals!" ~ Kuan Yin

126. "You have a lot more power and options for creating your world around you than you are now aware of. Don't allow mind chatter to bring you down. There is so much opportunity to accomplish things. Sometimes we limit ourselves." ~ Kuan Yin

127. "Immerse yourself in the beauty of the world. Begin with marveling at the beauty of nature. Art and music nurture and balance the self. Indulge yourself with every art that engages the senses." ~ Kuan Yin

Kuan Yin Buddhism

128. "Take shelter in the arts. Taste, touch and smell: anything that uses and appeals to the senses! There are, as other examples of creative outlets, the culinary arts and working with flowers." ~ Kuan Yin

129. "I understand now how busyness can be a real distraction, how it can create 'made up' realities. Being present means an absence of past and future. I'm seeing how bringing the mind into the present is the link to eternity and that true meditation is the acceptance of no past or future. I realize these are amazingly brave concepts, that there are only moments upon moments to be lived. It's almost inconceivable." ~ Lena Lee

130. "Focus on whatever positive trait you want to achieve, as you would focus on a musical note. Fashion your own personal symbols and interpretations, those that work for you." ~ Kuan Yin

131. "If enough people know about this, if every human being could recognize the power of "the Love and Forgiveness Principle" all consciousness on earth would change instantly. Indeed, thoughts can change the course of history. Sometimes, all it takes is enough people knowing about a certain concept." ~ Kuan Yin

132. "Your ego wants to believe you can fix him. Meditate on the fact that you can't fix him. What is strong is admitting you are limited, that you can only do so much. You can't do any more than anyone else is able to do. You need to say (to yourself and not to him directly) over and over: 'I can't fix you. I can't make it all better.' It's all about letting go." ~ Kuan Yin

133. "You must acknowledge and experience this part of the universe [the earth]. Karma is intricate—too vast. You would with your limited human senses, consider it too unfair. But you have tools to really, truly love. Loving the

children is very important. But love everyone as you would love your children." ~ Kuan Yin

134. "The reason pain exists is because of some of the choices you, as humans, have made. Humans always have a great freedom to choose." ~ Kuan Yin

135. "Loving people is the most helpful thing anyone can do. Your society has the resources, at this very moment, to fashion industries and lifestyles conducive to a non-harmful environment. There is a popular belief that over-population is the threat to the earth's environment. However, for many places upon the earth it is also very much a question of resource availability and distribution. There is a real need for creating a holistic infrastructure that can support everyone." ~ Kuan Yin

136. "Everyone creates realities based on their own personal beliefs. These beliefs are so powerful that they can create [expansive or entrapping] realities over and over." ~ Kuan Yin

Kuan Yin Buddhism

137. "A helpful mindset is simple-living and high-thinking. Science is constantly evolving. Keep up to date on the latest technologies. Be aware, set examples and create trends that will positively influence people's lives and the environment. As I said earlier, however, this is also a discussion about love and developing a greater capacity to love. It can help everyone." ~ Kuan Yin

138. "There's a balance that makes something holistic and in truth. What I am placing my hand upon is a dense conglomeration of stuck energy made up of certain ideas. Naturally, not all ideas are included in this energy. It needs certain elements, things sprinkled into it gradually. Having compassion for the 'untruth'! That is what's missing. I'm sending compassion into this rock. One needs to slowly add elements of insight to reach truth." ~ Kuan Yin

139. "It's a good time to ask ourselves to look at the lies we are telling ourselves. It's a time to

Kuan Yin Buddhism

examine our thoughts and the thoughts of the people of the world. Let us all reflect upon the 'great mix' of free will and karma. Reread the past chapters and ponder what I have said. Karma is intricate, detailed. One cannot dwell on only one particle of this great collective energy. Your life is but one frame of an entire reel of film." ~ Kuan Yin

140. "A person can forget that this life is just one picture out of the entire reel of the movie. They could be frightened of the pain because they don't know when it will end. But it wouldn't be so painful if one didn't fear it. Know this. You can go through disaster and I'll still be here. I'm here for you eternally." ~ Kuan Yin

141. "We're all one huge family, a great continuum. Don't underestimate the power of the love created in your homes and families. This love has an immense potency, the power to influence other's lives in a positive way." ~ Kuan Yin

142. "The earth is the most important experience in your evolution. Your existence is eternal. This phase of your soul is so important because you learn so much in human form." ~ Kuan Yin

143. "Do not believe that your humanity prevents you from being spiritual. Know that this earth drama doesn't mean spirituality does not exist on the earth plane. Try to be forgiving and objective when enduring your own earthly drama." ~ Kuan Yin

144. "Indeed, one's approach to one's own life drama can actually affect the outcome. That is, certain interactive strategies can render an ordinary drama, spiritual." ~ Kuan Yin

145. "Loving kindness is the most powerful force in the universe...it is potent even when displayed during the so-called mundane tasks of daily existence. It's so potent that if everyone could get into that mindset for a minute or even less, all consciousness on earth would immediately change!" ~ Kuan Yin

146. "I know the whole story. You're at page ten but I understand the entire evolution. In reality, it's already over. It's a dream. Remember? You're living a dream. It's very complicated to hold the dream and live the dream. You are learning the art of juggling the dream and the world of dreams. Nobody really gets hurt." ~ Kuan Yin

147. "Don't limit the brightness. Reach through the dark energy and grab it. You might see the smoke coming out of the chimney and you'll even see the smoky sky. You need to reach through the smoke and bring the light to you." ~ Kuan Yin

148. "I am making a path of breadcrumbs back to one's true divine and peaceful nature. Every historic period needs some breadcrumb-makers. It is difficult for some to hear the voices of the Divine Spirit. This may be because some are so invested in material things. I understand. I feel a deep compassion for these

human beings. Material things are a temporary relief from pain." ~ Kuan Yin

149. "Problems can be created when one is so obsessed with his or her own death, when one is too attached to their life. This attachment to a single incarnation causes the species to play out gruesome deaths. If humans knew they were more than just this life, they would not plunder the land, each other." ~ Kuan Yin

150. "Gather your questions together. *Meet* me with your questions. Ideas don't just float in the universe; they are linked together, related. If you don't have a thought I can't have an answer." ~ Kuan Yin

151. "When you wonder about it, it is the right time to pursue that issue and change a particular way of being in the world. Find some, maybe abbreviated, way to meditate upon me each day. Take just a moment to think about me. A small ritual to keep your connection with

me can be helpful. Even just acknowledging me; helps me to help you." ~ Kuan Yin

152. "Even a second of thought about me is very potent. If one could spend even a minute meditating instead of grand acts of devotion, it would be very powerful. No one has to commit to long, drawn-out rituals. I appreciate it, however it is not necessary." ~ Kuan Yin

153. "There are a lot of people who have enormous wealth. In spite of having material things they have a poverty consciousness. Wealth is a state of mind. Real wealth is not worrying about money. Rather, be focused on higher consciousness." ~ Kuan Yin

154. "There is no place to hide. All of those existing on the earth are in this together. People can immigrate to [perceived refuges] if they wish. However, it won't release anyone from the Collective Planetary Intention and personal responsibility to others." ~ Kuan Yin

Kuan Yin Buddhism

155. "Pious doesn't mean one has completed their karma. Sometimes the words 'good' and 'pious' can mean 'afraid of pain': that those energies staying away from the real challenges are more afraid of pain then of loving God." ~ Kuan Yin

156. "Not until one has experienced the 'darkness', which is really ignorance, is one spiritually complete. Ignorance usually means those individuals who are convinced of something that is not truth. It can also be an investment in a certain, limiting identity." ~ Kuan Yin

157. "Humanity is misunderstood. It's a powerful place to be when it is fully experienced. However, it is often underestimated." ~ Kuan Yin

158. "Things can shift. Something that is true one moment is not necessarily true the next. There are many invested elements: elements that can affect the outcome. Ultimately, the outcome

depends upon the individual's Free Will." ~ Kuan Yin

159. "Everyone wants to know the outcome, the end. However, there is no end, only seasons of life. We've all heard it said before. Certain events, for example a move or a divorce, can be like a death. There are other examples, of course. Rebirth, flowering, wizening and then dormancy: the springs, summers autumns and winters of our lives represent one's full cycle of seasons." ~ Kuan Yin

160. "A lot of spirit energies are coming in all the time. Soul evolution is linear for some, non-linear for others. Some jump around experiencing a variety of lifetimes. It's a way for the soul to develop compassion. This time I took you through the 'back door', the place where 'energies' (I don't refer to energies in a hierarchical fashion--as 'higher' or 'lower'), come into human form. They evolve from a different angle: down to up, with not much of a

'past'. Others have more experience." ~ Kuan Yin

161. "The confusion on earth is created by differing energies. Any clash between energies is a result of a 'better than' mindset. Sometimes the children are even dragged into this mindset and then there are awful consequences. What people need to remember is they are eternal beings and that they never die. However, don't let these events distract you from reality. Reality is always truth, knowledge and bliss." ~ Kuan Yin

162. "People have to ask, to care in order to see me! They must have an intention to seek. While I represent nurturing, compassion, I'm not like some of the other saints. Different saints and demigods assist different energies. They come to people in their differing forms and at varying stages of human evolution. There are any numbers of gods and demigods, endless compassion for those who wish to attain a state of consciousness—comfort beyond their current

level.

There are the lower saints as well. They are the beginning stage and may be closer to the human realm as they feel sorry for people. But humans don't need pity. They need empathy, detached compassion." ~ Kuan Yin

163. "Consciousness does evolve. Kuan Yin is assuring me of that. Now, I see newer energies, smaller orbs of consciousness. Kuan Yin is telling me they are like cells starting out..." ~ Lena Lees

164. "You can help teach the world about empathy. If you'd rather use the words 'loving-kindness' that's fine. Empathy or loving-kindness! They're the same. But remember, they're very different from guilt or pity. Having true empathy is to understand other's pain and suffering from a place of strength." ~ Kuan Yin

165. "While quite skilled, the windsurfer is nevertheless very focused on the elements around him. The windsurfer is focused upon

how to turn the sail. His question must always be, 'what am I going to do with the wind that is blowing right now?' There are the waves and the wind, seen and unseen forces. Everyone has these same elements in their lives, the seen and unseen: karma and free will. The question is, 'how are you going to handle what you have?' You are riding the karmic wave underneath and the wind can shift. Everyone must take what they see and deal with that which is unseen. Fall into the water!" ~ Kuan Yin

166. "Sometimes things are none of our business. A playground fight is a perfect example. Those participating in the fight have an agreement. One can stand back and watch and maybe even offer comfort. Those engaged in the fight however, don't have to accept one's compassionate offer. One of your lessons, Lena, is detachment. Don't become addicted to negative news. There are some who want to be in a negative space, misusing doctrines." ~ Kuan Yin

Kuan Yin Buddhism

167. "There are so many realities. This is a microcosm of the whole, just one reality. From your vantage point it appears cruel and inhuman." ~ Kuan Yin

168. "Don't pass along the beliefs and actions you disapprove of to your children. Loving-kindness is potent even when displayed during the so-called mundane tasks of daily existence. It's so potent that if everyone could get into that mindset for a minute or even less, they would blast into a great ball of light. Even the newest (smallest) energies would blast through." ~ Kuan Yin

169. "You need to have faith that the process is guided and correct, that it is ultimately good and that there exists a kind of cosmic steering of evolution, a reason for all of this. It's already finished! The past, present and future have already occurred." ~ Kuan Yin

170. "Kuan Yin was explaining how life circumstances are either karmic or voluntary. At that very moment she mentioned how She already 'knows the end of the world': how the 'drama is already over'. Somehow, I knew she wasn't being irreverent or flippant about the [Iraq] war. She just knows. And during that moment, in a flash, the physical pain I'd been experiencing was gone." ~ Lena Lees

171. "Sit down, Lena, and see what I'm doing," instructs Kuan Yin. "Once this instrument is correctly tuned and kept tuned, any amount of chaos won't matter, won't affect it." "Of course," maintains Lena, "this is Kuan Yin's metaphor for keeping the body chakras well-tuned. She's telling me this is a continuation of her message concerning the effects of sound and vibrations upon physicality. She is also saying that the power of sound (and pulse) is why music is so calming and comforting."

172. "It takes a lot of strength to have faith. The illusion of earth can be a distraction. Maya can

be amazingly seductive. It can make one think it is bigger than the cosmos, and dissolve everything you've spiritually worked for. All are equal in value. However, some don't always express themselves constructively. Sometimes they even bring others down with their words. No one's more special than anyone else." ~ Kuan Yin

173. "Kuan Yin doesn't want them [people emigrating from other countries] to abandon their ancient ways. She says they are carrying the cellular memories of their ancestors. So many of those from the Eastern Hemisphere carry, (within their DNA), the divine wisdom." ~ Lena Lees

174. "There is imbalance on the earth between the male and female energies. Balancing the male and female energies on earth through enhancing the Feminine Aspect is integral to changing the Earth Karma. Kuan Yin is showing me a thin silver blanket. Upon observing it more closely, I see that it looks

more like a transparent, silver veil. This is the symbol the spirits are giving me for causing the female energy to be enhanced upon the earth. Accentuating the female energy would help the environment, as well. While they are very dedicated to their mission, environmentalists should understand that implementing feminism first will create the kind of universal awareness necessary for healing and maintaining the environment. Without the predominance of the feminine element, all efforts will continue to be futile. Achieving this awareness will take many years, but it can be accomplished." ~ Lena Lees

175. "Kuan Yin is showing the mass of people. She states: 'Abundance beyond what you can see is the 'Mass'. It's from a much higher realm. The bodies represent other realms and what they are capable of. People can tap into the Mass. However, no human being is able to completely contain the entire Mass.'" ~ Lena Lees

Kuan Yin Buddhism

176. "Talk to the Elders. Talk to the villagers. The ancient rituals have been continuing for generations. Over time, the rituals have connected to the greater realms; creating pathways to the sky. All the realms are controlled by sound. That is the GREAT SECRET. The rituals have created channels that connect the earth with these realms. They are called the 'Channels of the Realms'. I have provided you with the new information (as told in "Oracle of Compassion: the Living Word of Kuan Yin") but you also need the ancient wisdom in order for the earth to be fully balanced. An important part of this is, of course, focusing upon the image of Kuan Yin. Sound vibration is carried through the DNA (cellular memory) to the next generations. The Elders know this." ~ Kuan Yin

177. "It is presently the advent of the arousing of the Feminine Spirit in the world. The earth will eventually be completely enveloped in the feminine energy because the male energy is

Kuan Yin Buddhism

burning itself out. Eventually even men will acknowledge this." ~ Kuan Yin

178. "What is largely missing in the United States is acknowledgement of the spirit of the Elders. And they won't be listened to again. Instead, this same spirit will be brought from other lands." ~ Kuan Yin

179. "Everyone looks to the United States for the latest knowledge; the latest trends. Therefore, the female energy has to somehow reside in the United States more predominantly than it does now. That is one of the reasons why the United States is increasingly becoming more racially mixed. This racial diversity will allow the Elder Spirits to filter in from other cultures (as this awareness is carried within their cellular memory). One step that really will help is the election of a female president. It is crucial that the males just being born see and experience that first hand." ~ Kuan Yin

Kuan Yin Buddhism

180. "Humans are multidimensional; able to divide their consciousness into several different places all at once while still being essentially unified. Depending upon one's personal needs and level of awareness, a person can go to another realm for further learning." ~ Kuan Yin

181. "I'm seeing a group of souls sitting in a circle. They are studying all the heavens; all the realms. These are realms that can be experienced or evolved to by the souls' consciousness." ~ Lena Lees

182. "It's all about consciousness—it's all about what a person was focused upon in their life. It's reflected on a different plane of consciousness and is what a person is attracted to. Hell is not a punishment. It's simply the reflection of a person's consciousness; someone who isn't very evolved." ~ Kuan Yin

183. "The first field of energy is the physical body. The spirit gets attached to the physical body. Thus, it is the first level of spirit. That is how

psychics and mediums can see and/or communicate with that particular manifestation of spirit. Spirit doesn't have to stay at that level, however. Anyone can evolve to other levels. One of the lessons of being human is that people are being trained to evolve to other realms. Yin wants us to know, however, that there is a kind of individuality within all the levels. Even though someone is 'One Force Always', they can be in the various realms simultaneously." ~ Kuan Yin

184. "Level two represents the earthly emotions. Level three represents the higher emotions (which one always carries within their soul). It is called the "Land of the Learning" and is a place many souls go after leaving their physical bodies. It is a very basic level. Those who are already quite enlightened can skip this level after passing over. Levels Five and Six are the Personal God Levels, for example, Kuan Yin and Krishna. They are the layers you can go to that are not of the material realm, they are called the Lilas. They represent levels of personal

experiences with God wherein you play a role. God can communicate with you outside of yourself—as if you were in a play. Your soul plays a role while also having an individual perspective that is comprehensible within the physical form. You can witness yourself in a dance with God. God has so many forms." ~ Lena Lees

185. "The physical body is very much formed by the emotional body. Additionally, the emotional body is very influenced by the mind. Enhancing one's level of spiritual wisdom helps elevate one's emotional level (one's "feeling tone") which is closest to physical reality. Thus, spiritual enlightenment is central to creating more expansive realities. In our present age, people are not exposed to enough of the spiritual light. The darker (ignorant) energies can be very seductive. Indeed, so many people have already been seduced and are now shuttered from the light. One way to open one's psychic being is to experience some kind of damage such as abuse, neglect or suffering. It's not comfortable.

Kuan Yin Buddhism

But it builds compassion. There has to be a certain percentage of the population having these kinds of experiences so there can be communication with the light. No one is compelled to stay in the darkness. There are now a significant amount of individuals who've been damaged in order to bring light through these damaged layers to the world. You have to bring in the light to heal the darkness." ~ Kuan Yin

186. "Kuan Yin is showing me an image of a field of seeds sprouting and water being poured on the earth. Now I see the seeds crack open and tiny green vines growing forth from the seeds. Of course it is a metaphor for planting seeds of Kuan Yin in the hearts of people and the bounty thereof: 'Even the non-believers will attain comfort from me!' exclaims Kuan Yin."

187. "Someone may not be able to completely forget the damage of mental or physical abuse. In that case they can only manage it. The whole point of choosing such a life path is to attain

compassion. There is a huge group of souls who are dealing with similar issues. They have freedom of will to react to it the way they choose. The aura 'holes' that can occur at certain Layers of Consciousness can be a source of alcoholism and other destructive addictions. People may want to numb the pain instead of sitting with the pain; being with the pain and then helping others with the pain. There are a tremendous amount of individuals on earth with this condition. The path, then, is learning to help oneself and then help others." ~ Kuan Yin

188. "There is a reality called the 'Place of No Worries'. It's a place where nothing happens. It's a very peaceful place that can be accessed through certain kinds of meditation. There is nothing here that can be deemed as good or bad. It is a place of neutrality." ~ Kuan Yin

189. "When a person crosses to the other side (having left their physical body), they can split up into different (multidimensional) planes of

consciousness all at once while still remaining as a singular entity." ~ Kuan Yin

190. "There is a certain level where a soul can just be an emotional body. In such a realm, a soul is not actually born. Thus, they do not have a physical body. It's not the highest realm. At this level, there is still pain and suffering. However, there are many who like to go here after leaving their physical body." ~ Kuan Yin

191. "The Land of Learning' (Level Three) is what many on earth call Purgatory. It is actually not a punishment, as some might believe. Instead, it's a temporary place where the soul can go to learn everything about the universe. It is also a place to process and heal any misconceptions or deleterious behavior the soul acted out while in an earthly body and where individual souls can go to process the karma from their earthly life. Most individuals souls (unless fully enlightened) have to come here to work on issues they had on earth and to acknowledge people they have hurt with their actions. An

Kuan Yin Buddhism

individual soul cannot progress unless they acknowledge the people they have negatively affected on earth. One can then skip this land and go on to the next birth. Some individual souls resist this land when they can't admit their defects of character. When this is the case they are attracted to a realm that mirrors their own energy. If their energy field is very dark they will end up in a dark place that reflects their energy. This can very well look like and thus be mistaken for a kind of hell." ~ Kuan Yin

192. "Your Being is a reflection of all the universes. Everything that is happening in the different universes is within you. You are already All That Is." Here is an image of the skin-encapsulated ego—showing how the human form is central to holding your infinite energy in place." ~ Kuan Yin

193. "Sound is what created the universe. Each of Level of Consciousness has its own sound and color—its unique vibration. When you hear the sound, you can see the sound. In musical

scores people are reading the code that accompanies the sound. The sound can then become a visual experience. The sound is perfectly tuned to the sound vibration at each of the Levels of Consciousness." ~ Kuan Yin

194. "If people can't see something, they don't want to believe it. The number of faithless individuals presently living on the earth is now more than any time in history. There are millions of people who don't believe there is anything beyond their physical/mental/emotional experience on earth. They don't believe there is anything beyond death. They don't try to understand that there is a greater reality. They don't believe so they don't try. Additionally, there are so many who constantly try to disprove the teachings that alternative realities, consciousnesses exist beyond death." ~ Kuan Yin

195. "I'm showing you pictures of people being treated unjustly. The male energy is way off

balance. The world is very sick. The yang energy is so prevalent that it could be compared to the white blood cells over-multiplying in the body. I'm providing images of millions of soldiers—even soldiers from the ancient past. Each person—each soldier is very special, a universe unto themselves. Each soldier is going through their unique process and that process must be respected. However, I say to you that the horrible sacrifice of the male energy is destroying us. Presently, in this paradigm, the male symbol represents this death and destruction." ~ Kuan Yin

196. "Everyone must send out prayers. Never forget to pray. Prayer is so powerful. The sound vibration from prayers travels; penetrates, when one prays mindfully. Study the rituals. There are those amazing Ancestors who've, through the eras, continued the rituals. While this spiritual pathway is usually enclosed and inaccessible to humans, the Aum chant can open the hole that can connect a human to the higher realms. Unfortunately, humans have

Kuan Yin Buddhism

lost their connection with the sacred languages which would allow them to easily connect with the higher realms." ~ Kuan Yin

197. "Here, I'm showing you a very elaborate necklace. There are prayers engraved on the dazzling gold jewelry. Several dangling, golden strands have prayers written in the same ancient language engraved upon them." ~ Kuan Yin

198. "There are millions of universes. There are too many to count. The universes or realms are infinite. There are no limitations." ~ Kuan Yin

199. "Higher beings—even simple higher beings, have many more senses than humans. Five senses are not very many. This is why most humans can't quite access all universal knowledge or memory of past lives." ~ Kuan Yin

200. "A soul will continue to have positive and negative experiences until altogether abandoning cycles of reincarnation to

ultimately return to Oneness—the One Force Always. The God Self desires to manifest and experience itself in all ways possible. God is neither male nor female. In fact, there is no pronoun to describe God. The individual is separate and not separate from God. One's life on earth is God's way of perceiving itself through endless manifestations; endless personalities. There is endless birth and death. Someone may forget that their life on earth is a Lila with God—a "dance with God". God says: *'Let me experience being the atheist. Let me experience being the doubter. Let me experience being the soldier. Let me experience being the thief!'* God is just trying to experience all the ways to manifest." ~ Kuan Yin

201. "I've said: 'There are the waves and the wind; karma and free will. Everyone has these same elements in their lives, karma and free will—the seen and unseen.' Karma is what someone has, thus far, created in their waking realty. However, someone always has the free will—the opportunity to change their beliefs and

perspective. Keeping you grounded in your earth reality, the ego chooses what it wants to believe and what it will focus upon. As one needs Focused Intent for manifestation, the ego is essential in the human manifestation process." ~ Kuan Yin

202. "It is your approach to your karma—your present situation, that determines an outcome. You have the power to transform your life right now. Just keep the channels open and have trust. If you can stay optimistic, any limiting life circumstance can be transformed. You always have the choice to keep the channels open; to connect with something greater than you presently believe yourself to be." ~ Kuan Yin

203. "Sending out loving thoughts causes the object you love to also experience that love. That is the magnificence of free will combined with focused intent. What you love, you become. What you fear, you become. What you resent, you become. When your beliefs change;

Kuan Yin Buddhism

when you redirect your energy in an expansive way, affirming your most expansive goals, everything changes. You are supposed to be attracted to and enjoy earth's beautiful and bountiful experiences." ~ Kuan Yin

204. *"The Path of Kuan Yin* emphasizes unconditional love; that which heals everything. All religion must eventually return to mysticism and the Divine Feminine. Every mystic has the same view and practice. The profound answers are found in mysticism. I cannot help unless one asks for my help. You've abandoned the earth plane. Instead of honoring the earth plane, Ascension from the earth plane is being taught. The earth must be honored as it is where souls learn how to be human and learn true, true compassion. Whoever follows the Path of Kuan Yin is following the path of compassion, love and forgiveness. The ultimate goal of the soul is going beyond being differentiated—going to Oneness. As humans, you are God's way of looking at himself/herself." ~ Kuan Yin

205. "You create your reality. If you think a certain thing, you will attract it. That is the Law of Attraction. Ego is a filter for attracting certain objects and events. It helps to maintain one's footing on the earth, as well. Ego is a profound teacher, showing us the patterns of our desires. Ask for what you want to manifest. However, don't be attached to the results. That kind of attachment can cause suffering." ~ Kuan Yin

206. "When you ask for something to be manifested you should say, 'Kuan Yin this is my desire. Make my desire in alignment with your desire.' Always check yourself. Too much ego can close one's ears from hearing the divine wisdom of the Bodhisattvas." ~ Kuan Yin

207. "You attract that being you have judgment (strong expansive or limiting beliefs and their accompanying emotions) of. Someone can attract entities that are reflections of issues

Kuan Yin Buddhism

they had in this or another realm that have not yet been dealt with." ~ Kuan Yin

208. "When someone works on their fear and anger, they can gain compassion. Fear always comes before anger. Still, many on earth will remain in their fear and anger until passing over. They have Free Will, so there is nothing that says they must heal their fear and anger. Yet, the ultimate answer is always compassion. While there are other realms having great beauty and intellect, it's much easier to become spiritually liberated in human form." ~ Kuan Yin

209. "Whatever name you call your God, the greatest mistake is to perceive God in a limiting way—that God is only interested in punishing humans. It is simply not true. God watches us as we destroy ourselves and says, 'I'm here for you'. However, people don't necessarily accept that compassionate offer. Kuan Yin (as a form of God) offers Her great compassion. And there

Kuan Yin Buddhism

is the Magnetic Force that always offers another opportunity." ~ Kuan Yin

210. "As a human, one may not be able to resist the lure of money, sex and power. However, even those seductive forces are there to strengthen your soul. The question on earth is whether you want to take the easy route or strive to develop yourself spiritually. There are realms where one can manifest whatever they want immediately through their thoughts. Of course, manifestation is not instantaneous on earth. This is one way that the earth realm teaches humility." ~ Kuan Yin

211. "Here on earth, you have the opportunity to hold in your heart and mind that even though you were severely injured you can still have forgiveness—unconditional love. This sacred earth experience is the only way to know this form of love." ~ Kuan Yin

212. "As humans, you are learning to be as compassionate as I am. Call on me and I will

help you to fully realize your compassionate nature. Just call on me and I will come. That is why there are so many statues in the world of me: beautiful, grand monuments in China, Korea, Vietnam and Japan; garden statues, fountain statues, alter statues and small pendants! All help people remember the importance of compassion!" ~ Kuan Yin

213. "Focus on developing your compassion and gratitude. Compassion combined with gratitude can heal. Such a powerful combination not only can heal any negative karma, it also attracts wonderful things. Such a practice can eventually attract more and more loving and comforting events to your life. Thus, you are not eternally-bound by karma." ~ Kuan Yin

214. "It's important to write down those events that you forgive and also those events you have gratitude for. When you write down what you forgive and appreciate in your life you are creating a Sacred Document. Often, the judgment of others and oneself is so strong that

only through meticulously listing what one forgives and what one appreciates in their life can the judgments and their resulting limiting karma be released. Write down what you forgive and what you have gratitude for and then read them out loud to yourself. Don't feel guilty if you cannot fully release your judgments. That guilt will only serve to bind you further to the original event you can't forgive. If someone can just try to develop their compassion and gratitude during their life, it helps tremendously." ~ Kuan Yin

215. "Make your home beautiful and decorate it with crystals. That is the way I can come into your lives even if you are not aware of me as a deity. It is a way for me to dance a little; to be playful. I love to be playful. There are rainbow prisms that emerge from crystals hanging in a window. I am the rainbow prisms dancing around the room. It's my favorite way to appear in the material world. Decorate your windows with crystals and you will see my living, moving

manifestation. Playfulness and laughter can help keep you healthy." ~ Kuan Yin

216. "Your memories are prayers. When you remember someone who's passed over in a loving way, such a strong, expansive emotion becomes a prayer that helps them heal. These same memories will also help those who knew and loved them, heal as well." ~ Kuan Yin

217. "Every Jiva soul has its group of angels to assist them in Purgatory. Angels sit across from a soul and act as a reflection of their life on earth. Any hurtful thing a person did during their life is mirrored upon the angels. Demons don't actually exist. However, when these reflections of a soul's hurtful deeds are mirrored in this way, it makes the angels look like demons. This in itself, then, becomes an experience much like Hell. In the end, however, these are only reflections, representing issues the soul has to work out. The soul is then asked, 'Which do you serve? Do you serve the

darkness; revenge? Or do you serve this angel of good?'" ~ Kuan Yin

218. "See my robe. See my beautiful light green robe! I love to dress beautifully. The jewelry you have on earth is actually a reflection of what they wear in the higher realms. However, they are living objects. All the jewelry in their crowns is living. In that world, they constantly compete for how ornately they can dress. They have so much fun! They do not call reality 'life' or 'existence'. Instead, it is simply called 'Presence'." ~ Kuan Yin

219. "How beautiful is the love of God! Remember the mystics of each religion. In any religion, you'll find the truth if you study the mystics. So many of the modern-day scriptures, however, are completely manmade. But the dogma isn't real. Humans have covered (camouflaged) the light and love of God in order to get permission to acquire things they want. Almost all the religions use the power of God for their own agenda. They try to cover the 'God Spark' by

projecting all sorts of things on that light and love." ~ Kuan Yin

220. "Find the 'God Gem'! There's a God Gem in every religion. However, it is often covered by dogma. God, in His/Her infinite mercy, has given humans Free Will and they, so often, chose the dogma. But it's not real. Attending places preaching heavy dogma could damage the soul. Ultimately, the dogma was intended to manipulate human behavior." ~ Kuan Yin

221. "There are vast generations (going all the way back through the ages to the origins of religion), that the God Gem has been filtered through. That is why it's so difficult to find the God Gem. God is trying to shine through the dogma. In spite of the dogma, there are many examples of the God Gem that have survived history such as the magnificent, beautiful creations reflecting the sacredness of that spiritual path. Indeed, its powerful influence has, over time, inspired the creation of, for

example, beautiful architecture and art from those who've followed this path." ~ Kuan Yin

222. "God is not dogmatic. Instead of judging God 'witnesses'. The concept of a Judging, Wrathful God is a limited concept interpreted by the limited human intelligence of certain ancient religions that are part of the age of Kali Yuga. Out of all the Yugas, Kali Yuga is The Age of Misinterpretations especially in religion. It is the age where the knowledge of God declines. The idea that God sends entities to hell is a misinterpretation. The Universal Law provides a place of intense purification. Burning is used in many religions and spiritual paths to purify. Creating a sacred fire for rituals is common in both Hindu and Buddhist traditions. In Catholic rituals, incense is burned to purify the church. Candles are burned in most spiritual traditions as a symbol of light; the light of consciousness. Notice how most all traditions and individuals just naturally light candles without even being conscious of what they are doing—that they are

initiating a purifying symbol of light (higher consciousness). God is all love. God is all love. You can face your fears because God is all love. Nothing you can do can turn Him/Her away from you." ~ Kuan Yin

223. "I will say it again. All will be well if people can just elect a woman president of the United States! Women need to come out from the shadows of men, as there is still so much oppression of women in the world. Indeed, many men were led astray. For so long, they've tried to silence women. Yes, much has evolved for women both in the United States and Europe. Yet, so much more needs to be resolved." ~ Kuan Yin

224. "There are no accidents! I want to discuss how the Spark of God is covered (camouflaged) by medieval practices. These practices don't belong in this realm anymore. Parts of the Bible were never intended to be continued and no longer belong in this modern era." ~ Kuan Yin

Kuan Yin Buddhism

225. "God has given humans Free Will. Humans are attracted to their judgments. These judgments create a specific reality that all people come together to agree upon. Everyone perceives what they want to perceive. It's always their choice! They have complete choice." ~ Kuan Yin

226. "You can meditate upon this beautiful burgundy-colored teardrop gemstone and know you are the God Gem. It's a place of wholeness where one can experience their divinity, their completeness and know their absolute perfection. Even if someone is covered by troubles, they will discover their good actions and thoughts are the pure gem underneath." ~ Kuan Yin

227. "Remember God is love. He/She wants you to know that love of God is the key. No one is judged for their religion. It doesn't matter what form of God you worship. Follow the lives of the saints in most any religion and you will find the truth. I report these things with absolutely no

judgment. They are transmitted with complete compassion. I only try to provide the facts." ~ Kuan Yin

228. "People want to know how best to worship me. If they pray for me, I will come to them. Nothing more, nothing less! You do not have to do the rituals." ~ Kuan Yin

229. "The 'magnetic force that always brings a new opportunity' has to do with abundance. There is so much abundance that people are not aware of. However, the wealth isn't distributed evenly in the material world. The source of so many problems on the earth is the imbalance created by 'need and greed'." ~ Kuan Yin

230. "People have Free Will. However, there is so much selfishness and greed on the earth. It's keeping things out of balance. Excessive materialism is so often a result of a certain belief. The belief is that if someone has enough material possessions, they will serve to hold

them to the earth and the person won't die. There are many wealthy and famous people who are terrified of death; who believe that money and fame will defy death. There are those who can become so dependent on having wealth that materialism becomes their God." ~ Kuan Yin

231. "It's fine to buy something if it makes you feel good. However, do not allow yourself to be consumed by materialism. It's very important that your energy field not become too cluttered by materialism. It can become a distraction from hearing the voice of God and can keep you bound to the earth. One does not have to live in abject poverty to gain saintliness, though. Some people do better in life if they have some material items. Thus, one does not need to completely renounce the material world to be saintly." ~ Kuan Yin

232. "I'm showing you what the earth would look like if every living soul was liberated. There would be an incredible, blinding light that

Kuan Yin Buddhism

emanated from the earth. Indeed, you do come to heal the earth. In your own natural evolution, you heal the earth." ~ Kuan Yin

233. "Don't blame yourselves if even after you think positive, expansive thoughts (intending to attract expansive situations) and then something disappointing or even unfortunate happens. For, self-blame is a judgment. Indeed, a limiting judgment (whether projected outwardly or inwardly) will only attract the same. Be the 'Watcher' (and do not judge) whether witnessing one's own or others' personal dramas." ~ Kuan Yin

234. "Remember, expansive or limiting 'karma' is but your present manifestation of prior thoughts and actions. Each and every person has Free Will to change their present circumstances and heal their life by affirming those beliefs and qualities that will best serve them. I repeat! No one is bound by negative karma." ~ Kuan Yin

235. "Everyone has the power to see the *lesson*; understand the belief responsible for both expansive and limiting manifestations. Beliefs and their corresponding emotions are the building blocks for one's reality. These 'blocks' can be rearranged according to one's preference. Perhaps you were carrying blame for yourself or others. Perhaps, then, cultivating more forgiveness is the key. Or maybe you didn't appreciate and affirm the gifts you receive every day, such as good health, family, friendship and the abundance that abounds everywhere. Examining any limiting thought patterns you may have carried from other periods of your life (for example, from childhood or adolescence) allows you the power to correct any limiting thought projections. You can pray to me or another Higher Power and ask that you be given the next right step. You can ask that you be given teachers to light your way or maybe a book or other material that will help us lead you from confusion." ~ Kuan Yin

236. "Each person has their unique Lila—their dance with God. That's what they want. That's what they do to themselves. The mystics broke out of that Lila. If enough people want it, they can break free from the punishing Lilas. They have Free Will. They can consciously choose. If enough souls choose a more liberating path, then the earth will no be longer conducive to a God of Anger; a God of Punishment; a God of Revenge. Lena, you're not obligated to play that Lila. No one is.! It's just the way it is. It's their personal relationship between their angry God and them. It's very personal. Don't judge their Lila. Be humble." ~ Kuan Yin

237. "The Timeless Truth is that prayer is so powerful! Send them love to help them through their ordeals. If it is a "Pure Love Prayer"; if it is unconditional prayer having no religious agenda, then you can pray and send love for their protection. Much healing can result from such a prayer. The following prayer is an example: 'I'm praying for you—that you will find freedom, growth and happiness and that you

will be safe from torment. I'm sending you this unconditional love.'" ~ Kuan Yin

238. "Coming to earth is a great sacrifice for souls. Earth is a training ground. Here, a soul can learn about the negative energies—that they can appear to be good, but can play tricks on you unless you learn to recognize and become aware of them. Some people have been so damaged. All kinds of addictions originate from certain false allures promising happiness and peace. For example, the lure of drugs and money can draw someone in and then leave them empty; craving for more. Those who make false promises are teaching us certain lessons; especially the lesson that one doesn't have to be terrified." ~ Kuan Yin

239. "First and foremost, God is love! It's fine to do rituals that help you remember there is a loving God. It's time for love! Whatever happens, it's always about love, forgiveness, compassion and gratitude!" ~ Kuan Yin

Kuan Yin Buddhism

240. "You don't have to become the storm. You don't have to absorb the storm. You just observe the storm. It helps a great deal if a person can stay in that love and compassion consciousness on a daily basis—doing some kind of ritual involving forgiveness and gratitude—holding the space for others who are seeking truth." ~ Kuan Yin

241. "A handful of souls are taking too much because they're fearful and they don't want to share. They've forgotten that what they need is within themselves; that they don't need to grab or hoard material items. They don't believe they have anything but their human condition. They spend so much time trying to disprove there is anything but what is visible to the naked eye."~ Kuan Yin

242. "People might behave badly. They might even hurt you. Beneath any ignorant or angry façade, however, is 'Soul Core Essence'. You don't need to judge it. Just observe it. Focus on what I teach. Focus on love. You can stare at

Kuan Yin Buddhism

the word 'love'. You can write the word 'love'. You need to actually become what I teach." ~ Kuan Yin

243. "Worship the qualities of love, forgiveness, compassion and gratitude. Focusing on love, forgiveness and gratitude helps if you're having difficulty feeling love, safety, trust and confidence. You need to practice this. Worship these qualities; this pure goodness; this 'Code of God'. People will deny me. People will deny that I exist. I'm here, waiting to be called upon. I want to get the word out. I'm impatient about this. When communities are formed around such concepts, then you have the beginning of something very powerful. You can help endless souls. Everyone wants to be loved. That's all they really want. That is the human condition." ~ Kuan Yin

244. "If you can create a space in yourself to meditate on the good; on love, then you can hold the space of love and compassion for others to join in with you. When you practice

this you will gradually be able to more and more recognize negativity and not be influenced by conflict. You can regard them and say: 'Oh, those are the angels of the negative'. Not learning how to hold the space of love and compassion is the lazy approach. You just need to practice the above Focused Intentions. If you can achieve this kind of inner peace, you will be very valuable once you leave the earth plane and go on to other places, realms. Please always replace the word "evil" with the word, "limiting". When you accomplish these things; really focusing on love and compassion, you can then become a wizard." ~ Kuan Yin

245. "Come sit with this energy for awhile. It is an All-Knowing Energy. There is so much beyond an earthly existence; when we leave our bodies. There is so much work to do in these realms. There are so many souls that need help. I'm just asking you to send my message about this All-Knowing, limitless energy. Most people don't have the opportunity to experience this energy

while still in a human body. Don't you know that you can come here anytime?" ~ Kuan Yin

246. "The first step to healing is to know that you're forgiven! Then a soul can evolve." ~ Kuan Yin

247. "Make me more real so that I can remind people that I exist. When there are thought processes that invalidate me; when people don't believe I exist, it causes my Presence in the world to be dissipated. When people don't believe in certain things, these things will cease to exist. People are so focused on surviving that they often don't think of me. It's hard for them to remember. When people connect with me and bring me more alive, I can help them. When they acknowledge my presence, that's what makes it work. However, I will never force my memory on people. It's all a matter of Free Will. Free Will is very important. People have to have Free Will to exist." ~ Kuan Yin

248. "I want to give the people hope. I'm raining down my love and hope. More than love, the people need hope." ~ Kuan Yin

249. "The Universe is God." ~ Kuan Yin

250. "Here is a symbol of a giant sheet that fills the sky. It's just a small piece of the God Force because the God Force is so overwhelming in its presence. My energy is part of this God Force. The luminous material in the sky is All Love and this love is in everything! It is everywhere!"~ Kuan Yin

251. "I'll stay on the earth until every soul is accounted for. I'm here to help every single soul. Just ask! Just trust! Be patient! You're around for an eternity. Therefore, you have plenty of time to understand it all." ~ Kuan Yin

252. "Practicing prayer, meditation and even a sweet ritual opens the channels through the layers of Maya and goes straight to the heavens. This energy meets the heavens and

Kuan Yin Buddhism

then comes back down through the channel. Prayer is so powerful as it can create channels through the dense Maya cloud. It's just a karmic thing. Maya is a massive energy of karma. Someone may not necessarily understand this earth condition. There are souls who are here to burn off karma. There are souls who came to help. The earth plane is not a place of punishment and penance but rather it provides an opportunity to learn. Maya is like a container—a framework. The human condition allows for one's defects to be more apparent. One can burn karma off just by existing on the earth." ~ Kuan Yin

253. "I'm a power magnet. "The Knowing" is already within you because you have me. I'll open the hole and what you need for your life will pour into you. I've taken away the gelatinous haze; any obstacles to manifestation." ~ Kuan Yin

254. "Originally, royalty and clergy wore crowns and headdresses for the express purpose of

channeling this divine "Knowing" energy. Crowns were designed to contain the perfect balance of elements (gemstones and minerals) to serve as magnets, conveyers for this Celestial Wisdom. Before this, the Pagans worshiped trees; considering them to be direct channels between heaven and earth—the Axis mundi.'" ~ Kuan Yin

255. "There are places on earth where "The Knowing" is more intense. Mount Shasta, India and China are but a few of these Earth Power Points; energy points where you can be more open—where you can receive "The Knowing" in dreams or visions. Within these Earth Power Points and even above the earth's atmosphere (where the Maya is less dense), it is easier to communicate with the spirit world. That is why certain astronauts had spiritual experiences during their voyages." ~ Kuan Yin

256. "Those who received "the Knowing" and have passed over say, 'People need to be

Kuan Yin Buddhism

open to us. We can help you. There is this incredible *Source!* There are many people who are able to receive this wisdom. They don't necessarily have to believe in the spiritual world. They're receiving and practicing "the Knowing" without understanding where the information came from. In fact, they may never be aware or acknowledge this Source until passing over. Then, they will realize that all along, they were part of "the Team"."' ~ Kuan Yin

257. "There are literally crowds and crowds of spirit energies wanting to help people on earth. They've already contributed greatly to the vast store of scientific knowledge on earth; especially alternative energy technology such as wind and solar. They love those living on the earth, even when people don't believe in them."~ Kuan Yin

258. "Once the body drops away, the soul realizes its powerful energy; its electricity. It experiences various imprints of itself and all

of its lives before. When people describe a Near Death Experience, they often tell of how they experienced the love and bliss on the other side." ~ Kuan Yin

259. "When one is living an honest life, they have nothing to fear. Then you can connect with your favorite angel, spirit guide or healing energy. It doesn't matter who or what you want to connect with as long as your desire is to connect with your perfect community of souls. And as I've said, once you drop your physical body, everything is instantaneously manifested." ~ Kuan Yin

260. "People aren't supposed to ignore what may be interfering with manifesting a fulfilling life. Instead, they need to work with what the karma is trying to teach them. One can only do this by acknowledging that their unhappy circumstances were somehow created by themselves. Don't waste time blaming yourself! Concentrate on what your karma is trying to teach you. Don't ignore it. The more you can

Kuan Yin Buddhism

solve it, the faster you can grow. Don't feel sorry for yourself. Everyone has situations in their life they have to deal with. It's all about what you do with your karma. Ease into it—learn from it. This is a very important lesson that I want to teach. Understanding and dealing with karma is such an important problem on earth because people often believe they're victims and don't want to deal with it. Instead of dealing with it, they're always fighting with their karma. Always take responsibility. When someone doesn't deal with their karma, things will just pile up more and more. Most people just want comfort. More comfort; never discomfort! However, don't abandon the discomfort." ~ Kuan Yin

261. "My whole existence is based upon love and compassion. I will be sending my message of love and compassion long after you leave your body. I am eternal. Eternal! It is humorous that people regard me as only a statue. Why would I come to earth as only a statue? My statue is there to remind people of my living essence! If

you pray to me, I will come! I won't pressure anyone to love or worship me. They have Free Will!" ~ Kuan Yin

262. "The earth is a reflection of the highest (True) realm (the Dalai Lama, saints, etc.), a middle level; a level after that and so on. The earth actually reflects everything occurring beyond the earth realm. Throughout the universe there are the various realms inhabited by populations reflecting a single specific value. It is on the earth, where these many and diverse replica realities (the Divine, Lila, Demigod etc. realms) manifest. The amazing thing about this earth reality is that all of these unique, mirrored realms exist here at the same time. The earth; a playground for tremendously diverse points of view, is not necessarily supposed to improve or be healed. As humans, you have the opportunity experience all the different levels and points of view so that you can choose who and what you will serve. You have absolute Free Will to choose." ~ Kuan Yin

263. "Just remember, that those who perform atrocities are already in a self-made hell. There is no need for them to go to hell. They're already within their own hell! I can't emphasize it enough! People have Free Will to choose their actions. There are levels of dark realms one will gravitate to, depending upon the consciousness of the individual after leaving the material body." ~ Kuan Yin

264. "These layers of dark realms are also represented on the earth plane. There are also several levels of "teaching realms" depending on what souls are prepared to learn. These are represented on earth as well. They are the neutral realms moving up to higher platforms of knowledge. There are millions of planets where both light and dark reside depending on the consciousness of the entities living there. There are endless heavenly realms as well. In some of those realms we can act out Lila's (our dance) with God. The highest realm is where we become one with everything and completely merge. Once reaching the Lila realms with God

or reaching the realm where we are One with everything, humans need not reincarnate any longer." ~ Kuan Yin

265. "I see a visual of a thermometer or thermostat. It's a diagram for the many, many Energy Fields of Consciousness. A realm where all Energy Fields of Consciousness are made manifest, earth is described as being at 'level zero'. Above the earth level zero are the ascending, ever more concentrated and expansive Energy Layers of Consciousness. Below level zero are the descending, ever more concentrated and limiting Energy Fields of Consciousness. The lower levels are nothing to fear; as each person has Free Will to choose their own path. God let's them do what they want. God loves souls so much that She/He gives them Free Will; letting them choose their own path. All personal experiences (even suffering) are completely controlled by the individual. It's important to avoid associating with those who've made limiting personal choices. Just pray for them! God loves

everyone. He/She wants people to have what they want! People are attracted to specific Energy Fields of Consciousness reflecting their personal values; that it really is the Law of Attraction!" ~ Kuan Yin

266. "There is the freedom on other planets—the freedom to be in any reality just by your thoughts. There, you have the ability to read another being's thoughts and the freedom to move things telepathically. This is found in other higher soul planes of consciousness. You who are human, who once experienced that ability in another existence, crave it now." ~ Kuan Yin

267. "Live always in the now. It is all you have. Thoughts create feelings which create emotions. Identify the distortions in your thinking. This will take some soul-searching. But if you check your distorted thinking and use the tools that have been provided herein, your experience of reality will be illuminated. Check yourself if you are stuck in greed and, with that energy, trying

to manipulate the future. There is only the now to work with." ~ Kuan Yin

268. "The word "guilt" has its own physical look. Hear me when I say: 'Stop blaming yourself for something you can't control!' I'm holding the mirror and asking: 'What are you projecting? What are you projecting? Look at you judgment. Look how a projected judgment can create entirely false images!' The stories people create and then project will be magnetized back to them. Acknowledge that many of the stories you are projecting aren't fact. The point of all of this is to objectively regard the parts of yourself that need purification/healing. Discard those pre-conceived ideas and stay in a place where your cup is empty. Practice that! If you can come to our sessions together with a blank slate, my Presence, will come to you in a much clearer form. You might even want to visualize sitting in a lotus position and meditating on an empty cup. When you approach these sessions that way, my messages will be much clearer. Humans like to blame a lot. They blame first.

Kuan Yin Buddhism

Blame of others and self-blame is apparent in so many religions. You need to take responsibility for your thoughts. Doesn't it feel better when you take responsibility? It will free your soul!" ~ Kuan Yin

269. "Remember, have an empty cup. Stop projecting! You might think you're expanding the knowledge, but you're limiting it by your pre-conceived ideas. Just clear yourself. Be in good conscious. Be of the highest mind. Do good works and be detached with the result. You need to adjust yourselves to the higher mind." ~ Kuan Yin

270. "Kuan Yin is riding a white dove," Lena describes. "I hear Her say, 'You know that the dove stands for peace. I want you to write about what you've learned about sound and creation.' I see Her now riding the white dove and flying above a beautiful Jade-green sea: 'The dove is the symbol of peace flying above the Jade River! I'm going to visit the people who are grateful. I want to know what makes people happy. I've

Kuan Yin Buddhism

given people a way to live by my message,' Kuan Yin concludes. "Kuan Yin," further explains Lena, "has an ear specially designed to hear gratitude. Off She flies on a dove of peace on the Jade River."

271. "Remember what the Buddhists say, "Chop wood, carry water!" Have an open mind. Take responsibility for what you create and what has befallen you.'" ~ Kuan Yin

272. "Every human day I change. As you know, I am revered for my shape-shifting; my many forms. Some say that I have thirty-three unique forms; each having their distinct meaning. However, there are many more than that." ~ Kuan Yin

273. "The message of the white hawk is that I can randomly send it to tell people what to say to change someone's life. It's exciting when a human can talk to one another and change their life! Don't you agree? I am sending a hawk to change a life in an instant! I so enjoy, indeed

love, watching when someone talks to another and changes their life!" ~ Kuan Yin

274. "Every living energy has their own God Power; their unique expression. Even the tiniest ant has its own unique expression. The range of unique expressions is so vast, it can't be counted. Every living thing has its own life force. Even every ant walking in a straight line up a wall is unique. It's important to know that the ant before and after the ant climbing that wall is completely unique. Thus, it is impossible to live and not influence something else. This is unavoidable." ~ Kuan Yin

275. "There are those religions that focus on not wanting to harm anything. Yet, obviously certain violations are impossible to avoid. Indeed, many of these affronts are not intentional and therefore accrue no karma. The original intent is what matters. You might not understand the reason for your circumstances. When your karma pushes you in a certain direction, it's important to learn from the

people and circumstances surrounding you, for they are a mirror showing what you must learn. Observe it. Don't resist it. If you don't believe you deserve your karma, you can say 'what can I do to improve this situation?' Some karma is big and the hurt is there for a specific lesson. Just remember, God is expressed through everything. God says, 'I want to dance with this person and that person. So let me dance with them through their experience on earth." ~ Kuan Yin

276. "Suffering is a choice! Work on understanding what you can and cannot control. Focus on the miracles and the knowledge. There is endless, endless knowledge around you. It's so much fun! I know you enjoy it. Just continue to focus on the knowledge. It's a heavenly practice!" ~ Kuan Yin

277. "Just pass over the books and other media that offer only knowledge of hatred and destruction. Ignore them! Everyone has a need and sometimes those needs are offensive. Be

endlessly open-minded, though. You will gain so much when you open your mind. There is the Bible saying: *'The Kingdom of God is within you!'* Most people don't realize they can access this knowledge; this "Kingdom of Heaven" within themselves." ~ Kuan Yin

278. "I'm in such an expansive mood today. I'm here today just to remind you of expansiveness. Remember expansiveness! People close themselves off too much. That's the whole problem with them. It's so boring! It's so uncreative! It's so repressively boring. Everything exists! Artist, performers, inventors! They know this. Everything you could possibly think of exists! The most exotic animals anyone could dream up exist in other realms. Just enjoy that thought. There are endless possibilities—endless choices that one can follow in their life. You have the freedom to follow this path or that path to learn of endless reactions and outcomes. Approach your life with the best attitude so you can create the best outcome." ~ Kuan Yin

279. "Have the best attitude and lots of gratitude! You wouldn't believe what you can create with just those two things! By the way, there is an actual realm where the hawk exists." ~ Kuan Yin

280. "God/Universe does not want you to limit your expression. Preferring to manifest in all ways possible, God/Universe is expressed through the individual desires of people. God loves enjoyment—loves to play with the individual souls that are a part of the God Force. The reason for suffering is that souls forget they're a part of God. When someone tries to live their life apart from God, they create negative karma. It is God's love to dance with people and their different expressions. Indeed, God is not against any of these expressions. It's difficult to comprehend God because God is everywhere and in everything. As the "Dancer", you should strive to be in step with God. Then your life will be perfect. Sometimes people want to be independent and

Kuan Yin Buddhism

try different things. Still, one can always go the 'God Way' which is defined as no intentional violation of others. Sometimes one's words or actions may unintentionally hurt others, just through free expression. Obviously, someone can be hurt if their mind is closed to new ideas. Such unintentional misunderstandings are not karmic. However, intentionally violating someone is dancing away from God. This kind of independence from God that may result in the intentional hurting of one or many people (such as in other lifetimes) can create negative karma. Gratefulness is the God Consciousness. When one is grateful, God will come to them because they are in the God Consciousness." ~ Kuan Yin

281. "There is the Wall of Gratitude. You know how Jade is considered a very special gem in the Chinese culture? The Wall is an almost Jade color, now." ~ Lena Lees

282. "There are things you can do to align your body—that each body organ has a specific

sound. In your present-day culture, there are many disruptive sounds—sounds that can cause your body to be out of alignment. You might wonder why certain people listen to, for example, music that you wouldn't necessarily choose to hear. When people are attracted to certain sounds, they are seeking some kind of healing. They have their own reasons for wanting to internalize the quality of a particular sound or music. Sometimes the sound or music is healthy for them; sometimes it is not. There is more information to be learned about sound and the other realms." ~ Kuan Yin

283. "Sound, music and vibration create all the realms. Sound can heal and even awaken certain potentials within us. Absolutely everything has a unique vibration and sound." ~ Kuan Yin

284. "When someone is not on the right path, they'll bump into obstacles. When things get wobbly, the universe is saying you're not on the right path. As far as the Law of Attraction is

Kuan Yin Buddhism

concerned, many miss that there is a correct foundation upon which this Universal Law must be built upon. It's important to write down all that you now have with profound gratitude. You wouldn't believe the abundance you already have. Take each and everything you have and meditate upon it. Send those things gratitude. Right now, someone is thanking me for their washer and dryer. Right now, a homeless man is thanking me for the sunrise. Right now, a fisherman is thanking me for his hot beverage. These are examples of the correct Law of Attraction foundation." ~ Kuan Yin

285. "There is a right way, a right path for the Law of Attraction: attitude, gratitude, choice and trust! Employing this way will assure the Law of Attraction doesn't become the Law of Materialism. In fact, there really is a Law of Materialism. Be careful! There is so much energy—groups and groups of people focused on the Law of Materialism. There are many souls trapped in it. Obviously, it can be

Kuan Yin Buddhism

pleasant to have nice things. However, many souls become trapped in their own materialism. The truth is that focusing only upon material objects takes a lot of energy. So it's important not to have too many material things. Try to live simply. Someone would not want too much of their energy field taken up with materialism." ~ Kuan Yin

286. "On the other hand, you don't need to harm yourself with self-created poverty. Some may choose the path of a monk. Certainly, that's one pathway to enlightenment. It's a way to realize one's identity and move on from this incarnation gracefully. In many ways, it makes it easier for a soul to leave this plane of existence." ~ Kuan Yin

287. "Thoughts create reality. However, certain Law of Attraction teachings are overly-focused on materialism. One's attitude and choices greatly contribute to what they will ultimately create. Approach the Law of Attraction from a spiritual perspective. Actually, very few people

Kuan Yin Buddhism

utilize this approach, opting for a "quick fix" for their problems. Something is mistaken for a get/get. When forgetting gratitude it can quickly become a lose/lose proposition." ~ Kuan Yin

288. "Keep in mind that there is an enormous population on earth that will never have the comforts that so many Americans have. Cherish what you have every moment of the day. If you want to attract someone or something into your life, observe and be grateful for what you already have! If you want another career, observe and be grateful for your present career. If you want your first car or another car, observe and be grateful for your present form of transportation. There is a river formed by thoughts of gratitude. It's a river of possibilities—endless possibilities!" ~ Kuan Yin

289. "There are endless possibilities to build your story around. Refrain from building your story on only one way of thinking. Open up your psyches! Refrain from worrying or thinking

Kuan Yin Buddhism

there is only one possibility or one solution." ~ Kuan Yin

290. "The bright white light is always there for you to relax into. Just a little of the white light every day can relieve your suffering! It will help heal your heart chakra and solar plexus. Don't forget to enjoy the beautiful, heavenly place where you live. Take walks in the forest and observe the beautiful trees! Each day, you have the opportunity to take walks in the forest or on the beach. It's a youth elixir when dancing and playing in nature!" ~ Kuan Yin

291. "Surrounding yourself with like-minded people is very healthy for the mind. Conversation with those who are supportive keeps the mind active. Having an open mind; exchanging ideas with people with interesting perspectives and from different backgrounds is good for body, mind and soul. There's a certain wholeness that can come through when interacting with others. People's auras can actually touch each other when they are in a

supportive group. When auras merge, people can attain healing from others' auras. It can keep you young and is very healing—especially in musical groups. There is an exchange, a great convergence of power. Gain energy through trusting others and trusting in their goodness!" ~ Kuan Yin

292. "The First (the physical body) and Second (emotions) Levels of Consciousness are earthbound. However, the Third goes with you when you leave your physical body. The emotional bodies involve the mind as we are such emotional beings. And the emotional layers actually support the ego. So when you have certain levels of damage, your body is often aware that it is not fully intact." ~ Kuan Yin

293. "Level Four: the Ethereal Body. When one passes on, the physical body leaves an imprint on the soul. The soul will tend to emulate the physical body, thus there will be an ethereal body that is identical to what the physical body looked like during the soul's life on earth. This

Kuan Yin Buddhism

is how psychics and other living entities are able to contact loved ones once they have passed on and physically recognize them."

294. Level Five: The Ethereal Intellect. One can access knowledge from the ethereal brain. One is still aware of their own consciousness after leaving their earthly body. Knowledge of past lives is accessible. Decisions can be made with this ethereal intellect. There is an ability to understand beyond what one was capable of in the earthly body from the mind's imprint of ideas on this subtle body. Here, one can tap into the "Essence of Thoughts" one had as a physical being. It's a realm where one understands that knowledge extends beyond the human brain, merging with the Cosmic Mind; the Celestial Wisdom. Beings experience this level because God wants them to feel the essence of love. Within this level, one realizes the God Force was with them all the while they lived their lives in their material body—that there is a God Force in every single person. The soul knows that Creation happened because God wanted to experience himself/herself in all

the various manifestations. The reason why loving oneself is so important is that the God Force loves everyone unconditionally; loves them exactly as they are. The God Force is "the Watcher". The God Force has absolutely no judgment whatsoever. This is such profound knowledge, as so many religions characterize God as judgmental or vengeful." ~ Kuan Yin

295. After a certain Energy Level of Consciousness, beings are not born. Rather, they simply become expressions of their former selves. They have the option to completely transform; no longer appearing as their earthly form." ~ Kuan Yin

296. "My message transcends any culture or nationality. We've got to get this path of love going. Be the Path of Love! Be it! It's all about love! Nothing else matters! Give love freely. Remember to give love freely. Your path is with us!" ~ Kuan Yin

Kuan Yin Buddhism

About Hope Bradford CHt

A spiritualist and hypnotherapist, Hope Bradford CHt has been profoundly influenced since witnessing and transcribing the Kuan Yin Buddhist parables as revealed in the book: <u>Oracle of Compassion: the Living Word of Kuan Yin</u>. It was during that time that Kuan Yin promised to appear again to Ms. Bradford—that they enjoyed a very personal relationship. Included in this latest work, <u>Kuan Yin Buddhism: Parables, Visitations and Teachings</u>, Ms. Bradford delineates her amazing dreams and experiences with this revered deity of the Chinese Pantheon—that in addition to the originally-set down teachings, the ancient wisdom continues to this very day!

At some point during the Kuan Yin channelings it was revealed that Hope's encounter and hence relationship with Kuan Yin was integral to Lena Lees Kuan Yin channelings: *"Hope, Kuan Yin sends you bands of energy. The bands look almost like the Milky*

Kuan Yin Buddhism

Way, where nebulae are constantly born. She sends these bands through you so that the wisdom can be spoken by me. We're a team. I can't do this without you! Now, I see Kuan Yin in such a beautiful form. Her countenance is such a brilliant white that there is a blue aura radiating out from Her."~ Lena Lees

"People want to know why I chose Lena and Hope to bring forth my message of loving-kindness to the world. It's alchemy! Lena and Hope's combined energy creates an open channel that I can manifest through. It is very rare in the world. It doesn't matter what nationality a person is. I can go wherever I want. I come to them because they are receptive."~ Kuan Yin

Kuan Yin Buddhism

Printed in Great Britain
by Amazon